The Best of
DICK SHEPPARD

The Best of DICK SHEPPARD

(H. R. L. SHEPPARD)

Edited, with an *Introduction* by
HALFORD E. LUCCOCK

HARPER & BROTHERS PUBLISHERS
NEW YORK

THE BEST OF DICK SHEPPARD
*Copyright, 1951, by Harper & Brothers
Printed in the United States of America
All rights in this book are reserved.*
No part of the book may be reproduced in any manner whatsoever without written permission except in the case of brief quotations embodied in critical articles and reviews. For information address Harper & Brothers

FIRST EDITION

M-Z

Acknowledgments

The editor wishes to express his appreciation to the following publishers who have granted permission for the reprinting of material from the books listed below:

JONATHAN CAPE, *What Can We Believe?* edited by Laurence Housman.
MESSRS. CASSELL & CO., *God and My Neighbour* by H. R. L. Sheppard.
HARPER & BROTHERS, *Impatience of a Parson* by H. R. L. Sheppard.
LONGMANS GREEN & CO., LTD., *Dick Sheppard and St. Martin's* by R. J. Northcott.
THE MACMILLAN COMPANY, *Two Days Before* by H. R. L. Sheppard.
METHUEN & CO., LTD., *If I Were Dictator* by H. R. L. Sheppard.
JOHN MURRAY, *H. R. L. Sheppard* by R. Ellis Roberts; and MOREHOUSE-GORHAM, *The Human Parson* by H. R. L. Sheppard.
ST. MARTIN'S REVIEW, *A Conspiracy of Silence, The World Need, Broadcasting, The Open Secret of Christmas, A Word to the Critics, The Sermon, A Sermon, The Need for Idealism.*

Contents

Introduction   xi

1. A CONSPIRACY OF SILENCE   1
   from *St. Martin's Review*

2. THE WORLD NEED   6
   from *St. Martin's Review*

3. CHRISTIANITY IS A TERRIFIC EXPLOSION   11
   from *If I Were Dictator*

4. IF I WERE DICTATOR   15
   from *If I Were Dictator*

5. IS THE CHURCH FULFILLING ITS TRUST?   20
   from *If I Were Dictator*

6. BROADCAST ADDRESS TO NON-CHURCHGOERS   24
   from *St. Martin's Review*

7. OVERCOME FEAR   28
   from *God and My Neighbor*

8. THAT "COMMITTEE MIND"   31
   from *God and My Neighbor*

9. THE POWER OF PRAYER   35
   from *God and My Neighbor*

10. ASK YOURSELF FOR A REFERENCE   38
    from *God and My Neighbor*

11. SLAY YOUR DRAGON   41
    from *God and My Neighbor*

12. THE VISION OF A CHURCH OF GOD   44
    from *Dick Sheppard and St. Martin's*

CONTENTS

13. A PASTOR LOOKS AT HIS PARISH — 46
    from *H. R. L. Sheppard*

14. IMPATIENCE MAY ALSO BE A VIRTUE — 47
    from *The Impatience of a Parson*

15. AN ADVENTURE RATHER THAN AN ORTHODOXY — 54
    from *The Impatience of a Parson*

16. CHRISTIANITY OR CATASTROPHE — 59
    from *The Impatience of a Parson*

17. "THE GALILEAN TOO GREAT" — 66
    from *The Impatience of a Parson*

18. THE SERMON: Preached at the Consecration of William Temple as Bishop of Manchester, July 21, 1921 — 76
    from *St. Martin's Review*

19. A SERMON: Preached at the University of Cambridge, May 29, 1921 — 80
    from *St. Martin's Review*

20. THE PARSON'S OPPORTUNITY — 86
    from *The Human Parson*

21. INTIMACY WITH JESUS — 89
    from *The Human Parson*

22. HIS VALUES AND OUR VALUES — 95
    from *The Human Parson*

23. ON PREACHING — 103
    from *The Human Parson*

24. "FATHER, FORGIVE THEM" — 111
    from *Two Days Before*

25. "I THIRST" — 117
    from *Two Days Before*

CONTENTS

26. "IT IS FINISHED" ... 121
    from *Two Days Before*

27. THE NEED FOR IDEALISM ... 125
    from *St. Martin's Review*

28. THE OPEN SECRET OF CHRISTMAS ... 130
    from *St. Martin's Review*

29. WE MUST NOT FORGET ... 134
    from *Some of My Religion*

30. THE MINISTRY OF ART ... 136
    from *Some of My Religion*

31. MUST THE CHURCH COMPROMISE? ... 138
    from *Some of My Religion*

32. SIMPLIFY CHRISTIANITY! ... 140
    from *Some of My Religion*

33. HUMAN NATURE CAN CHANGE ... 142
    from *Some of My Religion*

34. WHAT WOULD LONDON DO TO CHRIST? ... 144
    from *Some of My Religion*

35. THE LONELY ... 147
    from *Some of My Religion*

36. A WORD TO THE CRITICS ... 150
    from *St. Martin's Review*

37. RESPECT THE VIEWS OF THOSE WHO HATE PACIFISM ... 153
    from *What Can We Believe?*

38. HUMOR ... 155
    selections from *H. R. L. Sheppard; The Human Parson; God and My Neighbor; Some of My Religion*

39. SPARKS ... 161
    selections from *What Can We Believe?; The Impatience of a Parson*

Introduction

A canon of St. Paul's Cathedral, London, has recently startled the world with the information that the Cathedral is moving down Fleet Street at the rate of one inch every hundred years. "Dick" Sheppard thought that the Church should move faster than that! His life was spent in an effort to get the Church to move faster in the service of human need. The record of that life is one of the most gallant and stirring stories of the Christian ministry of our time.

H. R. L. Sheppard, affectionately known as "Dick" throughout Great Britain, was essentially a great spirit, rather than a preacher or a writer. Consequently, it is peculiarly difficult to convey his quality through any body of written work. For one thing, the total amount in print is small. More difficult by far is the task of conveying through print any adequate suggestion of the unique and radiant personality which made him one of the most trusted and deeply loved figures in the Church of the twentieth century. It is no exaggeration to say that no one of comparable prominence and influence left behind so little in printed form, and that no one left writing more worth preserving.

A picture in words, which comes as near to catching some of the quickening qualities of the man as any words could, is that written shortly after his death by one of the most skillful masters of English prose in this century, Sir Max Beerbohm:

It was at Portofino that I first met Dick Sheppard. . . . On men of my age a man who seems very young is apt to have the effect of making them feel older than their years. The Dean looked worn and pale but he radiated a youthfulness that was less than of an undergraduate than of a schoolboy. Nevertheless, he made me feel younger than my years. And better than my character. Generous, unselfish, altruistic. . . . In fact, I was under the wand of the enchanter.

My subsequent experiences of him were as my first one. It is a truism to say that he was irresistible. At any rate I never heard of anybody who did not find him so. His rays went circling round always in all directions.

At the end of Portofino there is a lighthouse. I often watch it at night, across the distance. And if at any time of night, I wake from my sleep, I am aware of a faint silvery recurrence of light upon the walls of the room: a friendly intrusion—"Ah, there you are!" Dick wore himself out with his years of far-reaching radiance in this world. Dick is gone. But the lighthouse remains, and reminds me of him.[1]

Two things in that tribute are particularly worth noting. One is the evidence it gives of the strong grip of friendship with which he held a person rather completely outside the world of the Church, a constant feature of Sheppard's life. The other is the perfect comparison to a lighthouse, scattering radiance in all directions.

A very different tribute, all the more real because it was not intended as a tribute, from a very different source, may be joined to that of Max Beerbohm. It was a remark made to Dick Sheppard during the first World War, by an irate woman parishioner of Saint Martin in the Fields. "What with the air raids outside the church and you inside, there seems nothing but explosions." A lighthouse and a series of explosions—Dick Sheppard was both.

No words can convey his self-evident sincerity, his insatiable interest in people and love for them, his reckless disdain of any barricade of red tape which kept the Church from the people, his hot impatience with lethargy and complacency, his humor, infectious as strong sunshine, his gallant courage, his devotion to Christ, which shone through everything he did.

When we remember that Dick Sheppard died at fifty-seven, and that during the last twenty-three years of his life, the crowded years of fullest achievement, he was laid aside about half the time by prostrating recurring illness, the sum total of accomplishment is amazing.

H. R. L. Sheppard—Hugh Richard Lawrie, to give him his full, resounding name—was born at Windsor, September 22, 1880. He was the son of Edgar Sheppard, a minor canon of Windsor. Three years later the father became Sub-dean of the Chapels Royal in London. The responsibilities of both of these offices of the father were connected, not with parish administration or preaching, but with music. So that Dick Sheppard was not a "son of the vicarage," yet his early associations did give him a familiarity with the world of the Church. He attended the Marlborough School for eighteen months. Popular with his

---

[1] Quoted in *H. R. L. Sheppard, Life and Letters,* by R. Ellis Roberts. (London: John Murray, 1942), p. 199.

fellow students, he yet had a miserable time there, largely due to the stupid cruelty and bullying of one of the masters, treatment that probably left a permanent mark in the feeling of inferiority and lack of self-confidence, against which Dick Sheppard fought all of his life. In October, 1901, he matriculated at Trinity Hall, Cambridge University, where he remained three years. His college years were pleasant, unmarked by any distinction of scholarship. The University seems to have made no deep impression of any sort upon him, and he gave no indication of what the future direction of his life would be, or of the character and personality which he later developed.

After leaving Cambridge a period of fumbling around followed, in which he tried to find some lead into his future work. Everything was hazy, except one thing—he would not go into the Church. Taking holy orders was to him completely out of the question. There was at the time, however, a well-established fashion or tradition of Oxford and Cambridge University graduates spending a year or two in a university social settlement in London. This tradition had gained great prestige through the work and persuasion of men such as Samuel Barnett, the founder of Toynbee Hall, Bishop Charles Gore, Dr. Scott Holland, Arnold Toynbee and James Adderly. On leaving Cambridge in 1904, Dick Sheppard decided to go and live at Oxford House in Bethnal Green, with the purpose of studying the conditions of the London poor, and possibly preparing for a political career.

It was at Oxford House, at the age of twenty-four, that the outward direction of his life began to take shape, and the inward growth began to reveal itself. In his work with boys' clubs and all the many relationships with the people of the neighboring slums, the quality which marked all his later years, his unreckoning expenditure of himself, was immediately manifested. Dick Sheppard never measured himself out with a medicine dropper. He gave full measure, pressed down and running over, a prodigal gift of heart and mind, time and strength.

The outward stages of his life and service are soon told. Dick Sheppard has been very fortunate in his biographer. The book, *H. R. L. Sheppard, Life and Letters*, by R. Ellis Roberts, is one of fascinating interest, a gripping story rich in detail and revealing letters. Reading it is a moving and rewarding experience. After a year as a resident of Oxford House, he became in 1905 lay secretary to his lifelong friend, Cosmo Gordon Long, then Bishop of Stepney. While there, he made his decision to go into the Church, and in 1906 entered Cuddesdon, a theological college, to study for ordination. In 1907 he returned to Oxford House as Chaplain, and in 1909 was elected the Head of Oxford House. In 1911 he entered the work of the parish ministry, becoming curate of St. George's, Hanover Square. He served at St. Mary's Church, Bourdon Street, and at Grosvenor Chapel. In November, 1914, he was inducted as Vicar of St. Martin in the Fields, at the age of thirty-four

With the name of St. Martin in the Fields, the name of Dick Sheppard is inextricably associated. He was later, for short terms, Dean of Canterbury Cathedral, and Canon of St. Paul's Cathedral. Yet few, if any, ever think of him as Dean or Canon. It was as "Dick" Sheppard of St. Martin's that he was known, for in that church he carried on for twelve years one of the most amazing ministries in the modern Christian history.

There was a time when the name, St. Martin in the Fields, was appropriate. The first church on the site *was* "in the fields." Today it has a quaint, poetical sound, as the name of a church at the very center of London, indeed at the very center of the British Empire. The "fields" in the earliest day were adjoining the monastery of St. Martin le Grand, at Westminster. The first mention of the church in any record is found in a decree of Stephen, Archbishop of Canterbury, in A.D. 1222. It became a separate parish in 1542 by order of Henry VIII. The present building was consecrated in 1726. When Dick Sheppard was inducted as Vicar in 1914, the church was practically empty, on the finest site in the world.

Then the miracle happened! The new Vicar transformed the church and soon filled it to overflowing. Indeed, the overflow often became a near riot, with the pushing of hundreds who could not get into the building. As one upset parishioner described it, "It may be hard for a rich man to enter the kingdom of heaven, but it is easier for a camel to go through the eye of a needle than for a parishioner of St. Martin's to get into his own church." Sheppard's own words describe in a characteristically humorous style the pressure of the crowds to get into the special afternoon Sunday services, which he started in 1915:

A lady wrote from the suburbs demanding a new hat and umbrella, both of which she said were destroyed in her attempt to obtain admittance to St. Martin's. The crowd and the crush were often vast around the church, but her adventures were scarcely believable. The lady avowed that she

INTRODUCTION xv

joined a queue at twelve o'clock beyond the Coliseum. She stood immovable till 2:30 when suddenly she was swept off her feet and carried right into the church and up to the altar rails. But much worse was to come. It seemed that with equal lack of reason the tide then ebbed, and "before I could get hold of the altar rails," she was swept nearly unconscious down the church, round the corner, down Duncannon Street to come at last to rest at the station house in Charing Cross, with dishevelled hat, broken umbrella, and, I fear, considerable loss of *morale*.[2]

There were many reasons for this drawing power of the church; yet they are all ways in which the spirit of the Vicar expressed itself. The interior of the church was brightened; it glared with light, a vivid symbol of the joy of the Christian faith and experience. The services gained a homelike, human quality, which conveyed persuasively an old invitation, "Come unto me, all ye that labor and are heavy laden, and I will give you rest." A remarkable inclusiveness in the congregation was evident, both in the appeal of the church and the preacher, and in the response to it.

Rich man, poor man, beggar man, thief, doctor, lawyer, merchant, chief were all in the audience. R. Ellis Roberts, in his biography of Sheppard, describes this inclusiveness in words of moving eloquence:

Hundreds of thousands of men, for whom religion had meant routine, boredom, mumbo-jumbo, something desiccated and dead, found it exciting, moving, helpful, alive. St. Martin's Church became the church of the classes and the masses; the church of fellowship and privacy; the church for the cheerful and the church for the desperate; the church for the healthy and the sick; of the young and old. It was a church in which the congregation was no more shocked at hearing the minister pray for the street walkers than pray for schoolteachers, for crooks than for the clergy, for blackguards than for bishops, no more shocked than when the Vicar laughed and told a funny story in the pulpit. It became a refuge for the unhappy and the home of the homeless. In short, it was a Christian church.[3]

The services and activities of the church were unconventional, in the high use of that word, meaning that they were not stricken by the paralysis of a dead tradition. In the early years of his ministry at St. Martin's, Sheppard had ringing in his ears the shocked cries of "Stunting!" from the prim protectors of routine and respectability, to whom any departure from the accustomed was blasphemy. Yet it was

[2] *Ibid.*, p. 100.
[3] *Ibid.*, pp. 92-93.

soon made abundantly clear that the whole interest of Dick Sheppard was deeply and profoundly religious. For him the center of the ministry of the Church was found in the Communion Service.

But just because of this deep religious devotion, he had the courage and initiative to employ all the resources of the Church and its fellowship to the meeting of human need, which poured in such flood tides through the center of London. During the war the church became a place of refuge to the thousands of soldiers passing through the Charing Cross Station just across the way, soldiers either leaving for the front or returning from it. The crypt was opened as a dormitory during the war, and kept open as a refuge for the homeless during the bitter years of the depression. A hostel, an employment agency, a guild of fellowship, the St. Martin's Players, a bookstall, a magazine of high quality, *St. Martin's Review*, broadcast services—all these and many more activities were means of ministry in Christ's name. Indeed, by its very location, as well as by its spirit, the church became, in a very real way, the living embodiment of Francis Thompson's vision:

> Shall shine the traffic of Jacob's ladder
> Pitched betwixt heaven and Charing Cross.

St. Martin's is located at Charing Cross. It was, for a great host of people, a ladder to heaven.

Perhaps the most accurate description of the man whose spirit shaped and shone through all these activities is to be found in the words of Dr. Lang, Archbishop of Canterbury: "Dick Sheppard burned his way through the world of his time in a consuming flame of love." Burning one's way through the world is a costly process, and Dick Sheppard truly burned himself out. He lived up ungrudgingly to the words of Robert Louis Stevenson: "Life is an affair of cavalry, a thing to be dashingly used and cheerfully hazarded." During his service at the front in the first World War, this report was made on him by an army doctor:

> He had no right to be so reckless, so stupidly careless of the elementary rules which govern fatigue and strain. He would identify himself with every dying man, and consequently he nearly killed himself. It was wicked![4]

That was his pattern all of his subsequent life and is responsible, in part at least, for the recurring breaks in his health. That reckless self-

---

[4] *Ibid.*, p. 84.

giving sprang from the deepest things in his life, his devotion to Christ, and his love of people.

His preaching was marked not so much by profundity or originality, as by a directness and simplicity, coupled with a desperate earnestness which gave it a peculiar power. He won and deserved that high accolade for a preacher, "The common people heard him gladly." A frequent result of his speaking was that which followed the first Christian sermon by Peter at Pentecost, people asking the question, "Men and brethren, what must we do?" He had a consecrated impatience with everything that blocked the way of people into the Church and into religious experience, ever ready to slash with a sharp knife the ecclesiastical red tape which he felt was wrapped around the Church until it became more like a mummy than a living thing.

Once during his years at St. Martin's, after he had written the book, *The Impatience of a Parson*, a book that came like hot lava from his mind and heart, he wrote to his friend, Lawrence Housman, that he felt that he would be compelled to leave the Church, because of his severely critical attitudes. Mr. Housman wrote back in violent disagreement, urging Sheppard to "Remain explosively within the church." That is a vivid phrase; and it describes exactly what Dick Sheppard did, he "remained explosively within the church" to its great benefit. In one place Sheppard says that Christianity is an "explosion."

Not even the briefest picture of the man could be true without stress on his humor. It was incorruptible, undefiled and faded not away even under the severest strain. It was true humor rather than wit, though he was a master of the barbed and pointed phrase. Its most notable explosion was in a contagious gaiety, often lifting the spirits of others when his own were at a low ebb. He could meet the final test of a genuine sense of humor—he could laugh at himself. He illustrated the deep relationship between humor and faith. When faith is truly strong, one can laugh about it and bring gaiety to it. It is when faith is insecure that the only reliance is solemnity. In many of his spoken words, on the fringe of his central, intense earnestness, there was a play of humor like heat lightning. He was never constrained by a fear of unconventionality, so that he could bring the full force of his unique personality to ministering to the minds and spirits and bodies of others. The remembrance of a matron of the Charing Cross Hospital illustrates this gift:

One day as she was going her rounds she heard peals of laughter coming from one of the wards. She walked along to see the cause. There was "Dick" Sheppard stretched out on the floor with one leg in the air. He was telling the patients a funny story and illustrating it with weird and wonderful actions. When the Matron asked to be let into the secret, he whispered, "When I came in here I felt that the atmosphere was rather heavy, and I thought they wanted a bit of cheering up. Laugh and grow fit, you know.[5]

Dick Sheppard embodied a startling group of paradoxes. He was extremely critical of his church in many of its actions and inactions, yet he was accepted by many of its strongest leaders and entrusted with such posts as Dean of Canterbury Cathedral and Canon of St. Paul's. He had a great hold on people completely outside the Church, yet without the slightest minimizing of the Christian faith and ethic. He promoted unpopular causes and did not lose his popularity. Thus, he was the most articulate and forthright pacifist of his time, yet the ties of friendship with hosts of people who did not share his views were never broken. He habitually aroused antagonism by his daring in the expression of his convictions, yet such was the affection with which he was held that bitter reprisals were absent. During all the crowded years of his life from 1914 on, his hold on health and life was tenuous and insecure; yet he gave the impression of abounding vigor.

From 1924 until his death in 1937, Dick Sheppard's life was one unending battle with sickness, punctuated with short periods of activity in designated posts. His difficulty was first bronchial catarrh, then chronic and acute asthma which never left him free for more than a few months at a time, and after 1930, heart trouble. He referred to himself as a "mouldy old crock." He was forced by illness to resign as Vicar of St. Martin's in 1926. The next three years he spent in a search for health in England, Italy, Canada and Australia. Yet during the time when in England, he kept going with a sum of work in meetings, organizations and radio that might well have laid low a completely well man. In May, 1929, he was appointed Dean of Canterbury Cathedral. He enjoyed the associations and the work. Of his work, when he could pursue it at Canterbury, Canon Campbell Crum of the Cathedral wrote, "His coming here was one of the best things

---

[5] *Dick Sheppard. An Apostle of Brotherhood* (London: Chapman and Hall, Ltd., 1938), p. 29.

that has happened to Canterbury since Augustine and his forty monks, or since those five or six Franciscans arrived, thirteen centuries or seven centuries ago." But he was so afflicted with recurring attacks that he was forced to resign in 1931. After three years, unattached to any post, but feverishly active years, he became Canon of St. Paul's Cathedral. He was never happy in that relationship. Though loyally supported by the sympathy and friendship of the Dean, W. R. Matthews, the struggle against the hardened traditionalism powerful in the Chapter, gave him a numbing sense of frustration in the realization of his vision of what the great Cathedral might be in the life of the city and all of Great Britain. He died in November, 1937.

The evaluation of Dick Sheppard as a preacher is a difficult task. He was not a theologian; not even, indeed, a logical thinker. He never made any pretension to learning or intellectual distinction. The written work which he left has no mark of intellectual brilliance. Just in print, he makes no deep impression. But preaching is more than print. Sheppard did exemplify Phillips Brooks' definition of preaching as "truth through personality." He also illustrated in a supreme way the significant addition made by Dr. Henry Sloane Coffin, "truth through personality *to a person*." Sheppard always talked to persons; he never merely sprayed the solar system with words. In that, lay his genius and his far-spreading influence. He had simplicity and directness; he was as clear as sunlight, his themes were basic ones of Christian doctrine and experience, even though his range in doctrine was far less than the full octave of the New Testament. It is not surprising that his preaching seemed deceptively simple. Many have even felt, "That kind of preaching is easy." The answer to that is in two words—"Try it." It is just as easy as great simplicity in painting. So one might conceivably say of the "Angelus," "Why, it's just a simple thing, a man and a woman standing in a field. That's easy!" Or of the "Madonna of the Chair," "Just a woman holding a baby. How trite!" It is a high art to be able to take elemental things and make them *live*. Sheppard did that.

Nor is it safe to take too readily Sheppard's own continual disparagement of his mental capacity. It should be remembered that his whole life was marked by an unjustified feeling of inferiority which caused him constant pain. Maude Royden has said of him:

I regretted it—[his inferiority complex]—because it gave people who had not one tithe of his intelligence an excuse for treating him as a golden-hearted fool, and this was a fantastic misrepresentation. Dick Sheppard not only had a first class mind, but was one of the widest readers of our time.[6]

He might be fairly called a "man of one book," for *The Impatience of a Parson* got far more attention than any of his other books. It exploded with a loud detonation, winning both criticism and applause. In its vigorous and cutting language, Sheppard pours forth his protest against lethargy and lassitude, against the sterile formality, and mouselike timidity which he felt in the Church of his time. The latter chapters of the book, from which no selections are included in this volume, propose changes in Church procedure and legislation. These are inevitably "dated," but the main concern of the book, its emotional drive, its plea for dedication to the weightier matters of the law, as opposed to a preoccupation with "mint and rue and every herb" is terribly "in date," thirty-five years after the book was written. *The Impatience of a Parson* shares much with an earlier impatience of a prophet who cried, "Woe to you lawyers also! For you load men with burdens hard to bear and you yourselves do not touch the burdens with one of your fingers," and who was angered when men turned the Temple which should be a house of prayer for all people, into a trading post.

Dick Sheppard was an ardent pacifist, perhaps the most effective and persuasive leader of pacifism in his time. Much of what he wrote on that theme is "dated" today, due to the turbulent changes in world conditions made by history since the 1930's. But pacifism is still a living issue and will be one as long as the Gospels continue to be read. He both spoke for and spoke to the conscience of the nation, and will continue to speak in years to come. As the leader of the Peace Pledge Union, he exerted an enormous influence.

His breadth of mind and spirit found expression in his work as National President of the Brotherhood Movement in 1935.

There can be no time limit to such intensity of sympathy, such a Christlike quality of love, such courageous vigor of witnessing, as shone in Dick Sheppard. He can easily be imagined as saying the words which Edwin Arlington Robinson puts into the mouth of John Brown:

> I shall have more to say when I am dead.

New Haven, Connecticut   HALFORD E. LUCCOCK

---

[6] *Ibid.*, p. 75.

The Best of
DICK SHEPPARD

1. A CONSPIRACY OF SILENCE[1]

The Anglo-Saxon is slower to confess his virtues than his faults. He will probably never find it easy to talk about his religion, but it should come a little easier than it does. "I should like to be a Christian like Father," said the small boy, "for then no one need ever know that I was one." Doubtless we know the story which the French poilu loved to tell of two Englishmen "from Oxford College," who were wrecked on a desert island; one rescued from the ship a barrel of butter; the other a sack of flour. They were, however, never destined to eat bread and butter together for, never having been formally introduced, they were unable to meet. The story, as a matter of fact, is out of date—it might have happened once upon a time, but in recent years we have become more forthcoming; what is perfectly conceivable is that two Englishmen in such a situation might have enjoyed their bread and butter while it lasted and lived together in great goodwill for many a long year, but that neither would ever have known if the other had any religious convictions. Of course, in the event of a death on the island each would have read over the other the Funeral Service from the Book of Common Prayer—a copy of which in novels and stories is usually washed ashore in readiness for an emergency.

I have no desire to make men garrulous on the subject of their faith. There is a conversational evangelism of an unnatural order which is very distressing, and yet I confess that I should like to feel that just now and then a man's religion might get out of control and run away with him—if not amok—giving itself and him away irrevocably. Christianity resembles love in this respect that it degenerates into a bloodless and lukewarm affair if it be never declared. The price of any vital retention is at least occasional expression. This

---
[1] From *St. Martin's Review* (London), March, 1926.

is no plea for religious controversy which makes conversation rather than converts, or for talk of an "improving" character which is often obnoxious and usually antagonising, but for honest reconsideration of that clause in the Englishman's unwritten creed of convention that runs "Thou shalt not refer to thy religion." Believing that Christianity is a movement and not a position, I am not therefore depressed about our age religiously nor about the changed attitude of men toward traditional religion. Behind much that is uncomfortable for orthodoxy and a somewhat undutiful eagerness to relegate to the cellar, without valuation, the household gods of their forefathers, the changes that men advocate are mostly in the direction of an increase in religious sincerity—for which God be praised. But these are not healthy days for mild and muffled enthusiasms—causes without passion are lost causes and no movement can progress unless it can count on the white-hot energy of its ordinary adherents.

At a time such as the present, when official utterance is suspect and there is little subjection to authority, it is unlikely that Christianity can be made to count unless its rank and file are prepared to play a more generous part in the matter of propaganda as well as of practice. It seems that English-speaking people have to decide whether or not they sincerely desire Christianity to prevail as their religion. If so, then those who decide the issue must really bestir themselves and put an end to that conspiracy of silence that makes it appear now as if the average layman would rather give his body to be tortured than allow his tongue to testify to the faith that is in him. In the East, where I write, Mahommedans are daily seen on their knees in public places at the hour of prayer—"most picturesque," we chorus together. In the West a man discovered at prayer in Trafalgar Square would assuredly be run in by the police—"most grotesque" would be our opinion in this instance. I am not advocating the use of Trafalgar Square as a prayer mat but making a comparison in the matter of public witness to religion between the "enlightened" West and the "unenlightened" East, which seems greatly in favour of the East.

Our reticence is defended by well-worn arguments—some more worthy of respect than others. There is, for instance, the fear of seeming a hypocrite that often dissuades men from mentioning their religion. We may respect this fear and yet point out that men do not refrain from advocating any other profession or interest that they have embraced on the ground that they have not yet attained to either competence or perfection. Also we make a grave mistake if we confuse the advocacy of Christianity with any implication of personal goodness on the part of the advocate. What men are asked to do is to let it be known that in spite of their own abysmal failures they believe that Christianity is the way of living that is most worth while attempting.

It is said, too, that a man's religion is his own business and no one else's affair. If that be true then at last we know why the Kingdom of God so obviously tarries, for in ordinary practical affairs we have never yet heard of anyone acquiring a business who did not forthwith talk about it, sing its praises and attempt to persuade all and sundry to accept it at his own valuation—indeed to do business with him. I imagine that liquidation would ensue on any other terms. If we segregate Christianity for treatment that would bring any other cause into the bankruptcy court we must not be surprised if it does not thrive.

Many keep silence from good words awaiting a more suitable opportunity. Sometimes—though by no means always—what we like to think of as tact is in reality timidity. We have to watch this tendency to postpone saying what we believe to a more appropriate occasion. An American Evangelist, whose religious phrases are not always ours, has recorded in his diary an experience which many would find to coincide with their own. "Never," writes Dr. H. C. Trumbull, "can I speak to a single soul for Christ without being reminded by Satan that I am in danger of harming the cause by introducing it just now. If there is one thing that Satan is sensitive about it is the danger of a Christian's harming the cause he loves by speaking of Christ to a needy soul." Our danger does not lie in the direction of outraging the laws of courtesy by inappropriate testimony, but in that of persuading ourselves that a later date will provide a better opportunity.

For the benefit of any who would like to bear their witness but do not know how or when to begin I would respectfully suggest that the best way to begin is to begin, and that the best time is (usually) now.

And lastly I would join issue with those who insist that the Anglo-Saxon is constitutionally incapable of speaking about the things that touch him most nearly. He cannot trust himself—so it is suggested—to reveal his heart's deepest interest. I wonder! Times without number I have listened while the young have spoken at inordinate length and with apparent and easy abandon about the someone who at the time most certainly represented their "heart's deepest interest": they have borne the strain of testimony remarkably well—better than I have. I have travelled from the city with business men; from the racecourse with lovers of the turf; and from clerical gatherings with my brother clergy; and so far as I could tell these men were returning from following the most absorbing interest of their lives, "the things that touched them most nearly." They did not appear to find it hard to discuss them—they talked naturally, glibly and even passionately; not once have I seen strong men dissolve into tears under the effort of unrestrained and public witness to their primary interests. Indeed I have sometimes been a little dismayed at the apparent inability of these friends to talk of anything else—they seemed too wedded to "shop." I have been in the Clubhouse when two golfers have returned from their game (misnamed a "friendly") to which their whole souls had very obviously been given; I cannot remember any excess of emotion even choking back the loser's flow of language as he explained how not even his skill could have been expected to triumph over luck so inordinate and so unmerited as that of his opponent. And all was spoken with an emotion that left no doubt that the loser was speaking of something that touched him most nearly. No: I must beg leave to question the belief that the Anglo-Saxon cannot trust himself to speak about the things he cares for most. I am inclined to think it is as true as that pleasant illusion of some teetotallers that wherever they travel abroad the water is undrinkable.

I wish it were possible to persuade men and women how much the cause of Christ needs their spoken witness. Perhaps there is nothing England so needs today as that those who set store by Christianity and wish it well should say so. There is a patriotism of time as well as of country, and every thoughtful man owes it to his generation to express his convictions on eternal things. If the rank and file continue to hold back, it must go hard with the cause of Christ; the harder nowadays since these are not times when the clergy are listened to gladly or readily. Without the witness of the laity Christianity will, of course, persist but it cannot prevail.

I am not greatly interested in denominational propaganda; I do not wish to see men prowling about seeking whom they may devour in the interest of their own particular way of thinking: I have no desire to hear the orthodox heavily compelling the poor bewildered stranger to listen to the incantation of formulae: but I do long to know that everywhere simple and humble men of God are standing by ready and eager—if occasion occurs—to tell gladly what power and joy the Lord Christ can give to living.

I fancy that opportunity would often occur if we would add this petition to our morning prayer: "Please give me a great deal of love and human understanding and, if it be possible, a chance of helping today for Jesus Christ's sake." I wonder if that prayer would ever be spoken in vain. I doubt it. All that I know tells me that if men and women would say it sincerely each day it would be answered before they lay down to rest. True, we might never know that we had helped; but then our work is of that kind that is not done well if we look for recognition or reward.

2. THE WORLD NEED[1]

We have been obliged in recent years, as Dr. Fosdick has reminded us, to contemplate the bankruptcy of an age which had some right to consider itself the most humanely progressive, the most enlightened and the most secure in all history. For the benefit of the many who appear already to have forgotten the horrors and crimes of the late War, which so grievously stained the reputation of our boasted civilization, let me quote from *The World Crisis*, by Mr. Winston Churchill:

All the horrors of all the ages were brought together, and not only armies but whole populations were thrust into the midst of them. . . . Every outrage against humanity or international law was repaid by reprisals, often on a greater scale and of longer duration. No trace or parley mitigated the strife of the armies. The wounded died between the lines: the dead mouldered into the soil. Merchant ships and neutral ships and hospital ships were sunk on the seas, and all on board left to their fate or killed as they swam. Every effort was made to starve whole populations into submission without regard to age or sex. Cities and monuments were smashed by artillery; bombs from the air were cast down indiscriminately; poison gas in many forms stifled or scarred the soldiers; liquid fire was projected upon their bodies; men fell from the air in flames or were smothered, often slowly, in the dark recesses of the sea. . . . When all was over torture and cannibalism were the only two expedients that the civilised scientific Christian states had been able to deny themselves, and they were of doubtful utility.

No one can accuse Mr. Winston Churchill of being a sentimentalist, or of here exaggerating the horrors of the Great War, and now, when thousands of young people in this and other countries are being

---

[1] From *St. Martin's Review* (London), November, 1926.

brought up to think of the glory of warfare, it is good that they and we should be reminded that in reality war is a purely bestial and devilish affair. We must not forget what has happened to the civilization in which we so trusted. Progress in science and education, and the increase of knowledge all round, have not fulfilled our hopes for them by making life safer and more agreeable for mankind: indeed with selfishness unsubdued man is as much more dangerous as his power for mischief and injury has increased. We are not to be trusted with this fresh acquisition of scientific knowledge. We cannot handle it either to the glory of God or for the welfare of mankind. Now that the ends of the earth have been brought together so that the world has become like a whispering gallery all that is likely for untamed human nature is a magnificent opportunity for a first-rate family quarrel. Even our higher education has its dangers; there is a sense in which in its purely utilitarian forms it can only do for men what the Devil did for our Lord when he took Him up to the top of a high mountain and tempted Him to make a bid for the kingdoms of this world and the glory thereof.

The progress and discovery of the nineteenth century from which we hoped so much have not saved us. The ancient races of the East have never admitted the moral superiority of the West, lately they have witnessed the spectacle of those to whom the world at large looks for the realization of Christ's ideals engaged in mutual slaughter. Is it therefore to be wondered that they remain unimpressed when we offer them the blessings of our civilization, or dare to suggest that they should become as we are, and welcome our merchant or our missionary? Have we any right to the assumption that a continuance of a civilization such as we have achieved, based upon force and competition, is essential for the welfare of the world? "The West," cries Gandhi, "has an unshakable belief in force and material welfare, therefore no matter how much it cries for peace and disarmament its ferocity will still cry louder."

As the cause of all our distractions Professor Bergson has suggested that our bodies have grown altogether too large for our souls. He says that the chief work of science has been to enlarge men's bodies: telescopes have enlarged his eyes, telephones (and now wireless) have enlarged his ears: trains, motors, aeroplanes have multiplied the speed of his feet, and guns have elongated the blows of his fist from two feet to thirty miles. "But what of his soul?" asks the Professor, and he bemoans the fact that all these splendid powers should be still in the hands of a generation that is little in moral stature. "The inmost necessity of mankind," he concludes, "is a spiritual life adequate to handle its new acquisitions."

Dean Inge has summed up the situation in a phrase. "It remains to be seen if civilization is to be mended or must be ended." And he goes on to add, "The times seem ripe for a new birth of religious and spiritual life, which may remold society as no less potent force would have the strength to do." By general consent some religion that can eat up selfishness must prevail. If we are to contemplate the future undismayed, worldly wisdom, even when supplemented by great good will of which today there is an unusual abundance, will not suffice, and we know it. But it would be unfair to suggest that we are to be influenced merely by considerations of self or race preservation. To do so would be to leave out of calculation the greatest of all the allies of religion, namely, the need for God in the soul of man. Men and women are "incurably religious"; they are haunted by divine things. It is the fashion nowadays to speak with anxiety about the future of religion as if there were grave doubts as to whether there was any future for religion at all. It is foolish talk. We may well be concerned as to the forms which the religion of the future will take, and apprehensive as to the fate of the various denominations in which we have attempted to confine it, but so long as human nature continues so long will religion, which belongs to the very nerve and tissue of life, persist. Today it reveals the natural and deep-seated instinct of men, who are coming to themselves after the insanities of recent years, to look back in longing to the lights of the Father's home where their true life belongs, and where the peace of forgiveness and the joy of sonship and the kiss of reconciliation and fellowship awaits them. Men do not use New Testament language today. They do not say, "I will arise and go unto my Father and say unto Him," but if they meet someone who is trekking homeward from the far country they long for the courage to bear him company. They do not question the wisdom of his choice of road, they merely regret the moral cowardice that dissuades them from a similar pilgrimage. It may be true that the modern man is not worrying about his sins, yet I fancy he is frequently worrying about his own moral futility and strange inability to carry through the good resolutions of the night before, which seems to me much the same thing.

THE WORLD NEED

I do not think that many, who have passed through the severe moral strain that the events of recent years have imposed, have emerged with a greater confidence in themselves and their own unaided efforts after betterment. Few thoughtful people nowadays can have an unbounded respect for their own character. It needs but an elementary knowledge of human nature as it is to realise that, if all our troubles and legacies of evil were suddenly removed by the wand of a magician and there was no corresponding change in the heart of man, it would not be many months before they were destroying and devastating our world once more, for the truth is that the world is as it is because we are as we are. The real tragedy is that there are so many people just like ourselves, no better and no worse.

There is little reason for complacence. Since the early days of the war the demands made upon the physical and mental resources of the human race have met with a glorious response both from women and men; not so the moral, here the supply available has not been sufficient to meet the demands. There are not enough Christians to go round. Everywhere there is a great readiness to die nobly, but little idea of living finely. Patriotism has come to be thought of solely in terms of war, though it has nothing to do with war, except for the hardness of our hearts, and the dullness of our understanding. Yet there never existed a greater number of better intentioned people. If we do extraordinarily badly we mean extraordinarily well. Of propaganda on behalf of good causes there is literally no end. The world is strewn with the literature of idealism, and we are perfectly prepared to give lip service to many of those ideas. But as George Eliot said "Ideas are poor things until they become incarnate."

A stranger who listened to our annual orations around Armistice Day would be vastly impressed. He would be singularly disappointed with their results. Armistice Day, if we are honest, has taken the place of Good Friday in the minds of most of the people in England. On that day we make noble orations, we talk about our noble dead and publicly assert our intention of paying the debt we owe them. The atmosphere is taut with the promise of great happenings and in the evening of the same day we all say what a great day it has been. But what really results? Hardly anything I think except the erection of some monument which would not have particularly interested the dead and which is wholly unlike anything they would have asked of England. They would have said, I think, "be juster, be kinder, let our death be the end of war, don't talk too much about us and don't pretend we were saints because we weren't: we were ordinary men like you who are left behind. If you must have a memorial do something that will enable our boys and girls to grow up with a fair chance of a decenter and more noble life. Give them greater opportunities for learning the art of living, and, where this is practical, clear an open space that they may play games and fill their minds with healthier things than now fill them by contact with the open air and the clean sport of young England. But above all do try yourselves to live nearer to those highest things of which we at our better moments were allowed a vision and let our young people be brought up to know the Christ who is bigger than any one Church."

We as individuals are primarily the disappointing factor: mercifully I fancy we are realising it at last. The good that we would, we do not, and the evil that we would not, that we do. We need the reinforcement of some power from without which will not merely censure our moral impotence but enable us to expel the coward and enthrone the hero that is in the heart of every man. We need something, some One, who can deal with this gradual paralysis of moral effort, which spasmodic resolutions of amendment on Armistice Day seem so powerless to allay. We need the God of Jesus Christ and His goodness.

3. CHRISTIANITY IS A TERRIFIC EXPLOSION[1]

The genius of English Christianity sometimes seems to consist in arranging Armistice Day services, or supporting the services at sea or on parade. I do not want to laugh at these manifestations of religion, but are they much in advance of Nationalism without any mysticism? Until we get mysticism or a Catholicism not steeped in Romanism, into our souls, we are not going to understand any gospel that can be universal. Christianity is not in possession. Without prejudice to the need for Churches it must surely be evident that those that exist are now incapable, if not unwilling, to express the values of God which Jesus Christ revealed. While religion attracts, the Churches frequently repel by their strange and inhuman attention to secondary and irrelevant affairs. The virile cannot be expected to take interest in most of the questions which Church people so frequently debate, since, whatever the result, the Kingdom of God will not be advanced.

It is impossible to suppose that the complicated forms which Christianity has so far assumed are any better than caricatures of what Christ intended. The Church Militant is not in fighting trim; indeed, it scarcely knows the difference between a battle and an affair of pillows in a dormitory. The "adventures" to which its leaders are calling it are, as a rule, ludicrously unadventurous.

The Churches, speaking generally, are half-hearted affairs not apparently engaged in any great business and no longer centres of attraction for heroic souls, who have always sprung from any society which has possessed a mystical passion. When mysticism is neglected religion withers, and mysticism is unfriendly to any and every form of authority—whether in the form of dogmatic philosophy or of a

---
[1] From *If I Were Dictator*, Methuen & Co., Ltd. (London, 1935).

dogmatic Church. Mysticism aims at the One behind the many, and the soul of the mystic cries out for the living God Himself, and the Church of Christ is meant to help men and women to find God, not comfort. What is wrong with the Churches is that they try to be both Christian and secular at the same time. Is not this perhaps to give to Caesar the things that are God's?

And yet all this does not excuse our empty churches, for it is not eloquent preaching nor beautiful music that men want, but a simplicity that is dignified, and sincerity that suggests that something wholly worth while is going forward. At the moment the Churches are primarily devoted to finance and prestige, and a great deal more sensitive to theological than to any moral issue. They have consented to enter the world's arena where the struggle for pre-eminence, from which most of our distractions arise, is fought with hate and fury. The Churches create and nourish innumerable men and women of good and saintly character, but corporately they do not count in the large affairs which determine the world's welfare. They do not put the fear of God into the cruel and rapacious, or the love of God into the hearts of the people.

They are for ever inclining towards that sin that their Founder so continually denounced—insipidity.

The long history of European Christianity [writes Dr. Zimmern], if it ever comes to be written, will be the history of a submerged and hidden movement—the tracing of the source of a pure but tenuous stream of living water, which has refreshed the souls of innumerable men and women who have penetrated to its secret recesses, but has seldom emerged into the open, to flow through the broad and dusty cities where the world's many activities are carried on.

The weakest spot of all is that we Christians do not really know what to do with Jesus Christ. We are sincerely devoted to Him, but not really convinced that a world "run" on His principles would be possible: surely what is needed is the Inner Light.

These charges I advance with sincere reluctance. I would gladly refrain from criticism, but I believe that the misery of the world today is the measure of the Church's timidity in former days to risk its life.

I see no prospect of amendment without grave disturbance, and I say there is no will or courage in high places for this. How can the rank and file be expected to be in advance of their professional leaders?

I shall be accused of gross exaggeration and hysteria, but I am convinced that this loud plea for a drastic reformation is sufficiently warranted to merit the most earnest attention on the part of the Church at large.

Nothing seems to me more futile, nothing more faithless, than to go on admitting in our souls that things have gone badly astray, and yet refuse to allow the evidence to be brought forward or critics to declare what actually the world must already know.

What is now needed is not that "discretion" so highly esteemed in ecclesiastical circles, but prophetic courage and simplicity, and above all a process of reeducation in the fundamentals of Christ's religion.

It is far too long since Christians rethought their faith and its expression. Empires have risen and fallen since then. It is time that we refused to give in to the prevailing disillusionment which breeds inertia and insists on being satisfied with what is, not because any one is really satisfied, but for fear of what might be if we moved.

I do not think the fire, which at any rate has cleansing properties, could be more unpleasant and destructive than the frying pan.

Never was there such a time for releasing the Gospel for the service of humanity as now.

The ring of confidence is lacking in the speech of all our wisest counselors. They know that the lessons of the past twenty years have driven home with overwhelming persistence, that our concentration on the things of this world is this world's most dangerous foe. Only if our abiding home is elsewhere can we be trusted to serve wisely here.

If the Church be not mystical—other-worldly, it can achieve nothing that is worth while. *"Just in so far as it knows its business and of what its spirit is, its centre of gravity cannot be in this world, though it is in this world that its task is to be performed."*

Christianity is a terrific explosion, lovely, violent, dynamic; it is Godlikeness, and its primary message is as a bullet that explodes in the soul of man. That is no comfortable business. Jesus Christ was not merely wonderfully kind and friendly to this world's failures. He was that and vastly more; a great deal of His teaching was spoken in the teeth of a mob howling for His life. It is not the Church's function to be content when it has taught men to be hearty and friendly and sociable. I yield to no one in the desire that Christians should "be kind to Granny and the cat." It is highly important that they should, and they are not good Christians unless they are, but kindliness is only one of the gracious implications and fruits that flow from discipleship and discipline.

Others are infinitely hard to fulfill since they entail the highest of all preferments—the cross—of a disciple who believes, but cannot always be confident in believing, that Resurrection follows, and that the suffering will not prove to have been in vain.

If we could recapture the sense of daring, mission, and spontaneity that characterized Our Lord's sure touch and which is essential for any who would take the humblest part in the world's redemption, then let the future be with God. What will happen need not give us one moment of terror or apprehension.

"I saw a great ocean of darkness and death cover the earth, but I saw a greater ocean of light and life, and it covered the ocean of darkness and death."

4. IF I WERE DICTATOR[1]

Recently I was told it was easy enough to criticize Church leaders for their timidity and lack of reforming zeal. All of us are brave in opposition, and it is not easy to put oneself in the position of a leader and know what one would do. Genius, I was told, will never submit to any form of dictatorship. That I believe to be true, but I will not believe all this nonsense about the genius of the Church of England. It is a frank misuse of the word to call it genius, but were the Church sufficiently wise or foolish enough to call in a dictator, I think I know what he ought to do. It is a wild supposition, at which readers will smile or perhaps shiver, but it is only fair to answer the question as to what I myself would do in the circumstances, and it requires a serious answer. Let us suppose, then, that the Church of England in a fit of desperation, and the noonday recognition of its spiritual inadequacy, were to ask me to dictate its policy.

With due apology for impertinence, here is my rough answer, into which I make no attempt to write the fear and humility that would be in my soul.

The word "dictator" irritates me. I do not like it, and would much prefer the word "adviser," since in the high matters to which I would be called, while I would be prepared to advise, I could not be prepared to dictate. To me that distinction is profoundly important. In the things of the spirit advice may be acceptable, but dictation from without is impossible and wrong. With this proviso let the dictator take charge for one month. In that span he could give all that he has to contribute. It will be a month of doing and not discussion. As adviser I shall not argue, but act, and when my time is over the Church

[1] From *If I Were Dictator*, Methuen & Co., Ltd. (London, 1935).

through its appointed channels must explain what I have done, or explain it away. In this way alone can I advise the Church of England: in demonstration instead of debate. But I must make one condition—my actions must involve, not Church people as individuals, but the Church as a whole.

For thirty days I must be allowed to represent the Church officially and with full power to act as I feel is best and right; unless this be permitted, in no circumstances whatever could I accept the offer of such a tremendous task.

We will suppose that my condition is accepted, and I am to be allowed to proceed—for one month. My action will not be the result of peevish impatience. It will spring from many a long year spent in thought and experience, and days innumerable spent in the wilderness, where often enough has it been shown in the past that great issues are simplified.

I am impatient and am not ashamed of it. As I wrote over ten years ago, "I have become convinced that it is the duty of those who have come to think as I do, no longer to exercise patience, but to speak out, not indeed with a blast of defiance or flippancy, but in a humble endeavor to assist where one may."

This obligation is not to be denied even to the lowliest working partner in a great concern. Christianity badly needs rash men who will not flinch from the crispness of religion, nor fear the result of stirring up wasps' nests.

There are times in history when decisive and courageous action is the only safe course to pursue, when it is high time that what is said to be desirable but impossible should be done, and done without delay. I am convinced that such a time for Christianity has arrived; that is, if it is to have any hand in persuading humanity to try the better way—God's royal road of love.

There is nothing more dangerous than to avoid danger; nothing so annihilating as timidity. There is such persistent and unwarranted patience displayed even by those who sincerely desire reform that I cannot believe there is need for one individual to apologize for a show of impatience for which indeed he is unblushingly impenitent. Why need we be patient if we believe the Holy Spirit presses on the hearts of men? We live in the dispensation of the Spirit, but it is scarcely to be believed; for, though we invoke Him constantly, we consistently ignore His arrival, at least if He bids us forget our un-Christian values and denominational loyalties. We prefer to sing the "Veni Creator" yet again, as if we hoped He might come next time with less compromising demands.

Forgive me if I appear to be repeating myself, but I feel the whole matter is so important that one cannot repeat it too often. What has happened in recent years? Almost precisely *nil* (the domestic reforms initiated by the Church Assembly seem to me to be spiritually negligible), and this only increases one's impatience.

I believe the programme that I shall submit is in the minds of the most thoughtful, and I would add the most sincerely religious men and women today. It is clear we cannot continue to "explore the situation" any longer: this blight of perpetual exploration is terrible. In a recent number of *Harper's Magazine* there was an article called "The Great Fact Finding Farce." The author ends: "How much more must we know before we act?" We must act, not (God forbid) because "something must be done," but because certain action is long overdue, and perfectly and obviously indicated.

As Dr. Whitehead has so aptly said:

The whole of our tradition is warped by the vicious assumption that each generation will substantially live amid the conditions governing the lives of its fathers and will transmit those conditions to mould with equal force the lives of its children. We are living in the first period of human history for which this assumption is false.

Why should the Church, I ask, be the last to realize this fact, and go on as if its medieval traditions should be all right for all time?

Here then is the programme I have to propose and I shall neither argue nor exhort.

What action should I take at once in the name of the Christian religion?

I should write to the Cardinal who is Archbishop of Westminster, to the head of the Eastern Orthodox Church in England, and to the President of the Free Church Council.

To each I should say that it was impossible any longer to believe that the disciples of the Father God of Jesus Christ could be justified in upholding any ruling that denied to each the right of full hospitality in one another's churches.

I should ask each to permit me to come unheralded to their Mass or Communion, and I should invite each to accept the hospitality of the Church of England in the same manner at St. Paul's Cathedral. Would the authorities respond? One certainly would, another might, and a third would almost certainly not.

But it is time that Christians despaired of their religion if it may not pursue the right course for fear of a rebuff to its prestige. I have never been able to understand the mentality of those who would bid their Church refrain from a good work for fear lest it meet with no response or give offense.

Next, I should rock the foundations of the establishment by declaring that the disciples of Jesus Christ may on no account take any lot or part in killing their brethren, white, brown or black.

I should stand here on what I conceive to be the Spirit of Jesus Christ, and I should refuse utterly and entirely to compromise. I might even add that I would rather see a nation go down into the dust of history by taking the risk of complete disarmament for conscience' sake than wax great in the glory of this world.

Since I believe in the establishment of Christianity as firmly as I disbelieve in the establishment of the Church of England, I should visit the Prime Minister and ask leave, in consultation with others, to nominate a commission to consider how the existing establishment could be enlarged and adjusted so that every approved Christian Church, if willing, could share with the Church of England the task of confirming and encouraging the nation in the Christian faith.

I should be prepared to pool the Church's endowments in the interests of other denominations, and if the loss of them enabled the new establishment to be entirely free to manage its own directly spiritual affairs, upon the necessity of which I should insist, I should not gravely worry to what financial stress the Church was reduced. Disendowment, part or entire, would not disturb my rest. I should hope that the larger Church that would arise would contain within its ranks a sufficient number of large-minded Christians who would do for it what the House of Commons has often enough done for the Church of England in the matter of saving it from the narrowness and bigotry which are the bane of sectional religion.

As a token that the Church of England had come to realize that the beginning and end of the Christian religion is the following of Jesus Christ in incorruptness, and that this may be achieved through other Churches as well as its own, I should put in hand legislation that would remove from the Enabling Act that most unhappy declaration required of voters for the Church Assembly, that they do not belong to any other religious body. That barrier ought never to have been erected. It requires immediate repeal.

5. IS THE CHURCH FULFILLING ITS TRUST?[1]

It is a fact that the majority of mankind are afraid of the truth. I do not mean by that that I consider "all men are liars"; far from it. In the ordinary affairs of everyday life they are the soul of truthfulness, so much so that sometimes they carry the obsession of truth-speaking to limits which are probably not morally justifiable. For the law of love is virtually greater than the law of truth-speaking, but in the realm of ideas most of us are afraid of the truth. This fact was vividly brought home to me a little while ago when a young woman, a graduate of one of our ancient universities, told me in the course of conversation that she was an atheist, and that she had no use for the Church. It was such a sweeping statement, made with such conviction and without the slightest intention of being ungracious. It could not be ignored, and the subsequent talk we had convinced me that if the Church was as she conceived it she and I were of one mind. Accepting what she had been taught, and then thinking out the problem afresh for herself, she felt that institutional Christianity had nothing to offer which could possibly help mankind to achieve the ideals she was so passionately convinced were true and necessary for the world's welfare. Those ideals were definitely based on the teaching of Christ. There are many outside the Churches who agree with that young woman. They get along quite well without the Church. They are alive to the needs of humanity, but they have weighed the Church in the balances of social necessity and leadership, and found it wanting. They fail to see what this insistence upon creeds and formularies and sacraments is doing to help bring about the Kingdom of God on earth, and they are not satisfied by being told that "right living is entirely dependent upon sound dogma, and when these innovators have had their little

---
[1] From *If I Were Dictator*, Methuen & Co., Ltd. (London, 1935).

day and beaten their feeble hands against the Church's granite walls in vain, then, as for ages to come, it will remain the repository of true faith, unshaken, dominant, and eternal." All this may be true, but it is also true that into the hands of the Church was given the spiritual leadership of millions of human souls. In what way is the Church fulfilling that trust, that duty to God and man? Are we not perhaps destroying the belief in God's goodness and love, a faith which through the ages has brought solace and hope and happiness to millions, and substituting a false God, a material travesty, a tribal idol created out of national vanity and lust for the retention of power and prestige? It is impossible to have faith in a thing in which we have ceased to believe, for faith is trust and confidence, and the Churches today do not inspire either. They have lost the Truth, or are afraid of it; indeed, on their own showing "they have lost the hearts of the people." "He that does not take up his cross and follow me is not worthy of me." "He that findeth his life shall lose it, and he that loseth his life for my sake shall find it." I suppose those statements meant something to Christ, and I expect the disciples were at first a little puzzled by them, but in the end they acted upon them. They ought to mean something to me and to you and to the Church, but somehow or other we seem to be doing nothing except cowering in our little trenches. Perhaps it is not entirely our fault. No one in authority seems to have bothered to make the words of Christ apply to the facts of life, we have been satisfied to rehearse the articles of our belief, but one has only to read the Gospels to see what Christ thought about most of the matters which our ecclesiastics think important. I admit they are important, but they are not important enough. Christ did not, I am convinced, mean to build up an ecclesiastical system. At least He spent a great deal of time in showing that the greatest religious system the world has ever seen was not bringing the people to God. In that respect He was following the tradition of the prophets. Christ was not interested in systems or creeds or dogmas, but I repeat He was interested in individuals and their latent possibilities, making quite ordinary men and women see the vision that He Himself saw, and live up to that vision. What difference does the Church make in the lives of many of its followers? Do we get that heroic passion for God? What difference do our Communions make? Are they making us more and more like Christ? What does the Church stand for in the world? Surely if anything for the principles for which Christ died.

The members of Christ's Church are those who believe that Jesus meant what he said—"I am come not to send peace upon the earth, but a sword"—signifying the strife for truth, righteousness, justice, and peace.

Once replace the word "Church" with the word "Christ" and we begin to see how far removed is the institution from that which Christ intended it to be. Is there not some justification for not believing in a Church which has forgotten the purpose for which it was made?

How can we be horrified at what we are pleased to call the anti-God campaigns, bad as we feel them to be, without considering whether the institutions that are being destroyed were in truth fulfilling their original purpose? How can we be annoyed when people say that religion is simply a drug to keep the people subdued to the things that are, or angry when states try to mold the ecclesiastical system to their designs? If men can find in the Church the living Spirit of Jesus of Nazareth they will follow, but can people looking for a sign find it today? Can communicants turn to storm-stricken souls and invite them to come and join with them in that sacramental feast because it makes them partake of the nature and life of Christ and become more like Him? And if we cannot expect them to do that what on earth do the sacraments mean? Is there any virtue in adding to our communicants if the world is not being made the Kingdom of Heaven? As I write these words assassination and murder are filling the political arena, and I ask, can the Church not do one single thing? To make our Communions, and not to be interested in slums, destitution, unemployment, war, and all the horrors that our civilization is bequeathing seems just a hollow mockery.

Where stands the Church in all these problems that cry to heaven for solution if not for vengeance? If it has a voice why doesn't it use it, or has it because of policy been stricken dumb?

It is probably true that if the Church did use its voice it would be persecuted. Well, Jesus was crucified. I can say no more, except that He rose again.

Our pride, our privileges, our dignity stand in the way, but yet how dignified was Christ when He denounced what was wicked.

Knowing what we do of Christ, can we today see Him as Pope, Patriarch, Archbishop, Priest, or Layman in any Church and imagine that things could remain as they are? And knowing and recognizing this, can we be contented and refrain from pressing for reform? It is not the revision of our services but a re-vision of our hearts that is needed. The Church seems to know all about Christ, but not to know Him. Christ was judged by His works, not by His orthodoxy. And is any other criterion of judgment necessary for the Church?

Men of vision will always know and follow Christ. It has always been so and will ever remain so; but the Church, as I said in a previous chapter, is in danger of losing that mysticism, that true devotion to Christ, which is the prerequisite of a true vision of His will. We are too concerned with keeping right with the world, to make the world right. The charming pagans of today are not satisfied where they are; they look to the Church for a leader, for real spiritual guidance, and often enough they look in vain.

Man is by his very nature a religious being. The soul of man cannot live empty of religion. Veneration and adoration of something higher than himself cannot be torn from the human soul. Man will worship something. It may be money, the State, power, knowledge, or God, but he hates shams, humbug, and hypocrisy. The Church as the Body of Christ could supply what man needs—the ideal, for the Crucified still stands as the symbol of the Gospel of love.

6. BROADCAST ADDRESS TO NON-CHURCHGOERS[1]

Anyone who is given the opportunity of broadcasting inevitably receives a large number of letters; this simple address is only printed in response to requests that have been received.

Many of you at this moment are wondering whether or not to put down the receiver: you do not as the phrase is "hold with religion" and its Church and Chapel-going and all the rest of it: the reason for this with a large majority is that you have so often come up against thoroughly bad examples of Christianity, and that has naturally put you off. This is not to be wondered at. If intellectual doubt has slain its tens, the Christian profession unrelated to practice has slain its tens of thousands.

The greatest problem of our religion is the unsatisfactory lives of professing Christians. There are not many who think Christianity through and then reject it on intellectual grounds, though of course some do; but a multitude pass it by because the lives of those who profess it do not square with the creeds they delight to acclaim.

I am not a betting man, holding as I do that it is the cause of untold misery and a fool's game besides. As to horses, I do not know a chestnut horse from a horse chestnut, and in that I am not unlike a million people who spend their lives backing losers. But were I to bet, I would wager that perhaps the majority of my unseen hearers this evening have said at one time or another this or something like this: "What's the good of religion, anyhow—it's mostly hot air and humbug. Look at So-and-So, he never misses his Sunday attendance at Church or Chapel, but it makes no difference on Monday morning, as you would know if you lived or worked with him. Psalm-singing humbug, that's what he is No, thank you, that is not the stuff for me." Let it be owned that

[1] From *St. Martin's Review* (London), August, 1923.

there are, alas, hypocrites in the greatest and most exacting of all professions, but it hardly seems fair to condemn Christianity, root and branch, because of its poorest exponents. We do not condemn other noble callings because their adherents are not as good in practice as they are in theory.

For studied and persistent hypocrisy in religious people I have no excuse, for the simple reason that there is none. There is nothing to be said about the Stigginses of religion except that the harm that they do is perfectly incalculable. There are no five men who have spoken against Christianity today in the Parks who have any power to hurt it equal to that which is hourly at the disposal of one professing Christian who is a consistent hypocrite. For such there is no excuse to be made, but only a prayer that God may have mercy on their souls in the day of judgment. I would beg though that the people who criticize and condemn Christians should make some attempt to distinguish between those who are wholly false to their profession and those countless other men and women who, while they are trying to be Christians, are perfectly well aware that they often fail, since the ideal they pursue is terribly difficult. These are not humbugs and hypocrites. Often they are brave men and women attempting a great adventure and even when they fail they are more noble than those who stand aside and criticize.

Let me tell you a story to illustrate my point. Once in France in the early days of war, before the time of conscription, I met a soldier returning in terror, bleeding and broken, from the front line. He had failed, I suppose. Later I heard him spoken to by a man who had never been within three miles of the German trenches. The vocabulary of abuse left nothing to the imagination. It shrieked contempt and ridicule at the soldier who had been in hell. I could not help reminding myself, and later reminding the man with the vocabulary, that in a sense he was not nearly so noble as his poor broken victim who had at least been in the front line, even if he had returned.

It is better to have loved and lost than never to have loved at all, and it is a good deal nobler to have tried and failed than never to have tried at all. Half the men and women today who, remaining at the Base, grouse at what is called the failure of Christianity would do well sometimes to remember that if Christians often fail, as God forgive us we often do, at least they are people who are aiming high. My friends, when you meet a professing Christian who is an out-and-out humbug, say what you will—short of condemning the whole of Christianity because you have met one of its meanest exponents. But when you meet a Christian, who is trying to follow the Master but sometimes failing, go a bit easy in your criticism, pause a moment or two to ask yourself if, with all his failure, he isn't perhaps a nobler creature than his critic: if only because he has been broken and battered in attempting an ideal higher than his accuser has ever had the courage to attempt. He may not stick it all the time, but at least he has been up in the front line making some effort and the scars that he bears are honorable.

And a word more if you will permit me. If in your homes or club or workshop you know a boy or a girl who is trying the great ideal that you so far have not attempted, don't laugh or jeer, but take off your hat and thank God that there are still a few idealists left in this old land. Maybe they'll fail, and be unable to hold on, but it were better for us that a stone were hanged around our necks and we were cast into the sea than that we should cause one of these little ones to stumble.

If you possess something nobler and truer than Christianity and have had the courage to stand by it, then you have the right to preach your Gospel, and God give you power in the preaching. If you have a more real person than Jesus Christ to offer men as their Saviour and Friend, then shout it from the housetops, for men desperately need salvation; but if you have nothing to offer that will save and redeem and make glad the heart of man, then for God's sake be careful how you criticize, with a view to destroying, the faith of those who have seen God in the face of Jesus Christ.

I grant that Christians fail; compared with what they profess they fail terribly: but if you can see that they are trying to make life happier for someone else and to live nobly and to fight injustice and cruelty and if you yourself have no alternative to propose, then at least wish them good luck and ask if a failing Christian, who is aiming high and falling short, isn't a good deal nobler than one who is aiming at nothing at all. Ask that until you have an alternative for the World's ills.

There is only one thing the matter with this old world of ours, and that is that there aren't enough practicing Christians to go round. Civilization is bumping from one catastrophe to another, and will so continue unless Christianity—the real thing—brings relief.

Man is incurably religious. When his life is noble he is haunted by God. So often the man who is haunted most is the man who abuses Christianity most roundly. He is asking so much of it really and it seems to fail him so often. The unsatisfactory lives of professing Christians are his real difficulty. He cannot get past that horrible stumbling block, and how well one can sympathise. Should there be one such listening in tonight, may I, a humble lover of Christ who often fails my Master badly, just say this: "For the Lord's sake, my brother or sister, come over and help us to be better—believe that we know how terribly often we fail: believe that we loathe the sorry mess we make of our lovely faith—that faith which was meant to run along the earth like fire eating up all that hinders the coming of the Kingdom of righteousness. If you have no alternative to offer for the salvation of men, if you have no friend to offer men more strengthening or compelling than Jesus Christ, then don't hold back because of our failures. Maybe we should do better if you were by our side. Maybe we should do better if you would give us at least the credit for wanting to be true to our ideals. Come over and help. No words can exaggerate how much the most virile men and women are wanted within Christianity if the soul of the world is to be saved. Don't laugh too loud at us. It hurts so much, for we know how often we fail. It is more noble to help than to criticize. Come over and help us for God and the World's sake."

It is so easy to criticize, so hard to create, so simple to sit in an armchair and say what others ought to do, but so difficult to get on to the platform of affairs. The world is as it is, because we are as we are. I am tired of the people who are always asking for their own rights and never remembering that what all of us need is not so much justice as mercy.

There was once a fashionable lady who went to a photographer. She was plain and thought she was beautiful. Said she to the photographer, "Young man, mind you do me justice," to which he replied, "Madam, it's not justice but mercy you need."

That is really our need too, and if we could see ourselves as we actually are we should know it and we should give up that perpetual remark of the complacent, "We have never done any harm." Many of us would discover then that our chief need was for Christ. The only hope of the world lies in a revival of real Christianity which shall include us.

This is a cry in the dark to over two hundred thousand people. Would God some at least would make answer.

7. OVERCOME FEAR[1]

You remember the old joke about the lion tamer who could overawe the fiercest of wild animals with a single glance and who went in terror of the little slip of a woman who was his wife?

It was always a good joke. Not because there is anything particularly funny in a man being scared of his wife, but because we're all afraid of something.

So, when we laugh at the lion tamer we are really, in a sense, laughing at ourselves—trying to convince ourselves that our own fears are groundless and unreasonable.

But fear isn't exorcised so easily. It is too deeply rooted.

It is one of the first emotions we experience on coming into the world. The baby is afraid—desperately afraid—of falling. That is why it cries when any one holds it who isn't accustomed to infants.

That fear never quite leaves us. Have you ever dreamed of falling through space? It is one of the most disconcerting of nightmares.

You awaken from it weak and trembling, hardly able to believe that, after all, you are really safe in bed.

As life goes on, fears multiply. They are, perhaps, foolish and unnecessary. That doesn't make them any the less real.

It's no good saying to a child who is afraid of the dark: "There's nothing to be frightened at." The child *is* frightened. Imagination peoples the dark with menace. It will go on doing so in spite of your reassurances. You can't reason with a child that is afraid. For fear goes deeper than reason.

Even now, perhaps, you are sometimes afraid of the dark yourself. A woman told me recently that, whenever she was alone in the house, she put on all the lights.

---
[1] From *God and My Neighbor*, Cassell and Co., Ltd. (London, 1937).

"I know it's silly," she said, "but I daren't even turn off the hall light when I go upstairs to bed."

Scientists sometimes explain this by what they call "ancestral memory." To primitive man night was full of perils. And we have spoken for centuries of "The Powers of Darkness."

All these things have a cumulative effect. Suggestion and tradition reinforce instinct. Besides, we feel helpless in the dark.

The sense of helplessness is at the root of most of our fears.

I don't know what your particular fear is. There are so many different types of fear abroad in the world today.

There are probably more people afraid of losing their jobs than ever before. There are always people who are afraid of illness.

Everyone who thinks at all about world affairs is today desperately afraid of war. I heard the other day of a woman who, during the last year or so, has been reliving in her dreams the air raid experiences of her youth. She can't understand why, after a long interval, these dreams should be recurring. But I think I can guess the reason.

There is a long catalogue of what doctors call neurotic fears. Many men and women are scared of any sort of responsibility.

They won't undertake any job in which they have to think and decide for themselves. Or, if they do attempt it, they have a nervous breakdown.

Thousands are afraid of marriage.

Whatever form our fear may take, if we face it, if we dig down to its roots, we discover that what we are really afraid of is ourselves.

We are afraid of life because we do not feel equal to its demands. So often we run away from it. We refuse to accept responsibility.

We let others do our thinking and make our decisions. We turn our backs on marriage. We avoid the society of our fellow men and women, and shut ourselves up in a private world of dreams and fancies.

But to escape from life is not to escape from fear. The harder we run away, the harder the pursuing feet come after us.

Courage is just as much part of human nature as fear. And the highest courage of all is to do what you believe to be your duty, even if you are afraid.

I said that was the highest courage. But it isn't the rarest. There are countless people doing just that today. Some of them are working beside you; there are others in your family and among your friends.

We all know people like that. They don't think that they are doing anything very wonderful. But they are a perpetual inspiration.

You can be like them. Every step that you take to conquer your fear, or in spite of your fear, makes the next one easier.

Love, too, is as much one of the fundamental human emotions as fear. And love casts out fear.

What are you frightened of? Nothing that you cannot conquer; nothing that you cannot overcome.

You may be weak. We are all weak. But there are open to all of us sources of strength that are sufficient for all our needs.

There has been some argument recently as to the efficacy of prayer. The answer to prayer depends, I think, on what we ask for. But I have never yet known of any man or woman who has prayed, honestly and sincerely, for courage and strength to serve the purposes of life, and who has not received them.

God still helps us to help ourselves. While we travel the road of duty, He will travel with us, and in His strength we shall be strong.

8. THAT "COMMITTEE MIND"[1]

Wickedness has gone out of fashion. Neither in fiction nor in real life are people bad any longer in the old whole-hogging way.

But it sometimes seems as if goodness has disappeared as well. We don't have contrasting black and white, only a uniform somber grey.

Well, human nature has always been a strange mixture. But past generations had the courage of their sins—or of their virtues—in a way that we haven't.

They did things—good or evil—off their own bat. They accepted personal responsibility for all their actions.

Today a great many of us are dodging that. We are trying to narrow down, as much as we can, the sphere in which we are directly answerable for what we do.

We can't, of course, evade personal responsibility completely. We must still stand on our own feet in our dealings with our family, our friends, and our neighbors.

If we break the law, and are found out, we must take the consequences.

But we live in an age of organization. And as members of an organization we sometimes do things which we should never dream of doing as individuals.

It is easier to be mean, or petty, or cruel, if we are acting in company with others. It is easier still when the victim is someone we don't know, who is merely a name on a works wages book or Case No. 199.

So we have the characteristic sin of the modern world—the sin of the committee man.

We don't, as a rule, recognize it as a sin. It doesn't interfere with our appetite or keep us awake at night.

---
[1] From *God and My Neighbor,* Cassell and Co., Ltd. (London, 1937).

If, occasionally, we have qualms we shelter behind the decision of the committee or the board. "The committee says so-and-so." "The board has decided"—these familiar phrases help to cover up our personal responsibility.

Or we work to regulations laid down by some other board or committee higher up. "We can't go beyond the regulations," we say, and proceed to interpret them in a narrow and legalistic way.

We've become part of a machine—and we're dealing with men and women.

This evil—for it is an evil—extends into every department of modern life. It even poisons the springs of charity.

I'm not quite sure when the phrase "cold as charity" first came into common use, but I think it must have been about the time of the original charity committee.

There's no coldness in the right kind of personal giving. It establishes a warm human relationship. And often the handshake, or the word of encouragement that goes with the material help, is the thing that counts most of all.

People who give in this way are sometimes "stung." But certain charity committees are so afraid of wasting their funds on the undeserving that those who most need—and most merit—assistance are either denied it altogether or suffer bitter humiliation before they get it.

I'm not saying that happens in every case. There are charity organizers who bring kindliness and human sympathy into impersonal giving.

But the big danger in our elaborately systematized benefactions is that we sometimes lose sight of the men and women and children we want to help in a mass of forms and statistics. The charity that is love is strangled by red tape.

All highly centralized organizations tend to go dead at the heart. There seems a curse of sterility on all G.H.Q.'s, whether in Church or State, business or charity.

Shut off from the current of common life, they issue their pompous edicts without ever trying to visualize what they will mean to the people affected by them.

Have you heard the story of the highly placed officer who, after the tragedy of Passchendaele had been going on for four months, motored out from general headquarters to visit the scene of operations for the first time?

As he saw the desolation of mud that was the battlefield—and before he had reached the worst of the swamp—he burst into tears.

"Good God!" he cried. "Did we really send men to fight in that?"

That's how the G.H.Q.'s work, whatever kind of G.H.Q. they happen to be. Only, as a rule, those who thus work havoc with the lives of others don't see the results they have produced.

There seems to be some malevolent magic about Government departments, public authorities, and big official corporations.

It doesn't sour the milk of human kindness—it just bottles it up and shuts it away during office hours. The people in charge are working on paper, and all they need for that is ink.

That, at any rate, would seem the only possible explanation of such things as, among others, the continuing tragedy of the Special Areas, the way in which the means test has been permitted to break up family life, and the ironic spectacle of villages where farmers daren't sell surplus milk to their neighbors at a price they can afford, and babies and expectant mothers go without.

But nobody is personally responsible—it's always the board, or the committee, or the department.

An M.P. once told me how, when a Labor colleague had become a Cabinet Minister, he took along a deputation from the East End to see him.

Replying to the deputation, the Minister never used the word "I." It was "the Board" this and "the Board" that. At last my friend could stand it no longer. He broke in:

"Steady, my friend. Try to remember the time when I was hanging on to the blooming Board's coat tails in Trafalgar Square, trying to keep it from talking treason!"

Now, that Minister was the best type of politician. He sacrificed his career for a principle. He is a humane and kindly man.

The truth is that, when we talk about the sin of the committee man, we're talking about a sin we all share.

We may not be members of any board or committee ourselves, but we've helped to elect them, or some of them, and we are content to leave them to get on with it.

We've got the committee habit. We don't see evil and suffering as a challenge to ourselves. We see it as a problem for a committee or a board.

But evil and suffering will go on, the world will remain a place of heartbreak and tragedy for millions, until we all realize that we have a personal responsibility for putting at least our own little corner to rights.

We don't want committees to tinker with humanity's troubles or to create new ones. We want in our own hearts the faith that moves mountains, and the will to get on with the job of shifting them as *our* job, and no one else's.

Believe me, there are mountains enough—mountains of misery and wrong—for us to move.

The essential thing to remember is the wisdom of the Founder of Christianity, who always suggested that people should think, not in terms of "cases" and "applicants" and "hands," but in terms of men, women and children.

9. THE POWER OF PRAYER[1]

Passing a teashop belonging to a well-known firm of caterers, a wit remarked that once the Christians fed the lions, but now Lyons fed the Christians.

It is really remarkable how familiar we all are, from infancy, with the idea of lions and their prejudice against vegetarianism.

To the very young it brings a peculiar joy, tinged perhaps with just a shade of delicious fear to give an edge to excitement. Play lions with a three-year-old, and your popularity is assured.

There are many references to lions in Scripture—more, probably than to any other wild animal. And we continue to encounter them in the records and legends of the Church.

Stories about them are recurring constantly in the lives of the saints and martyrs and—in modern times—of the missionaries.

The latest was published in the newspapers a week or so ago. It came from Rhodesia.

A missionary, it appeared, was walking through thick scrub to visit some of his converts when suddenly a lion jumped out from behind a bush.

This missionary was on foot, and the lion looked rather alarming as it lolloped toward him. Its intentions may have been amicable, but it seemed to him that the animal was in a temper.

What was he to do? He breathed a prayer and flung the Bible he was carrying straight at the lion. It dropped dead.

Recovering his Bible, the missionary returned thanks for his deliverance and resumed his journey. Rounding a corner, he found a man cleaning his rifle.

I have been surprised at the number of letters I have received asking me to comment on this incident.

---

[1] From *God and My Neighbor,* Cassell and Co., Ltd. (London, 1937).

"Isn't it rather a tall story?" inquire some of my correspondents. Others want to know if I think it was the prayer or the Bible that saved the missionary, or if the presence of the man with the gun was just coincidence.

It doesn't really matter how far every little detail of this story is correct. We needn't bother about that.

But what is interesting and important is the question it suggests to us. What is the place and function of prayer in our lives?

Prayer comes naturally to us in danger or emergency, or when we are in the shadow of illness or bereavement. At such times we turn to God as instinctively as a hurt or frightened child seeks the refuge of its mother's arms.

But are our prayers answered? Can they save us, for instance, from lions?

The Rhodesian missionary, very possibly, thinks that they can. Sir John Gayre, Lord Mayor of London nearly three hundred years ago, was very sure of it when he provided in his will for the annual Lion Sermon at the Church of St. Katharine Cree, which I was invited to preach last year.

Sir John had been shipwrecked. As he knelt in prayer a lion approached him, sniffed all round, and then made off.

In this case it may well be that prayer did save the shipwrecked man. But while he himself might have said that he was "protected" while he knelt, it was probably the unfamiliar attitude, the stillness and calm of the man who was praying, that first puzzled the lion, and then led him to look elsewhere for a victim.

To say that is not to belittle the power of prayer.

It was the sense of communion with God, that he had placed himself in God's hands, that gave Sir John Gayre the strength and courage to remain on his knees while the lion prowled round him.

In a similar way, even without the man with the gun, our Rhodesian missionary might have escaped.

The fact that he faced up to the lion, the unfamiliar missile thrown at it so boldly, might have disconcerted the animal and made it turn tail.

We *are* "protected" when we pray. We are "protected" in the sense that we are given new faith, new confidence, new courage.

It is in a somewhat similar way that prayer may help us in illness

THE POWER OF PRAYER

We pray for health, and sometimes—it seems almost as if by a miracle—health is restored to us.

There are many astonishing instances of this—examples of what is called faith healing. Belief in that is not superstition.

Prayer in cases of illness brings the patient into the frame of mind where he will receive the greatest benefit from the doctor's treatment, and in which the healing processes of nature are given their full value.

That, you may say, is something purely natural; we aren't entitled to say that it represents an answer to prayer. It *is* purely natural—but it is God Who is the Great Architect of Nature. This relation between mind and body is His handiwork.

And the strength and consolation that we derive from prayer do come from God. I believe that He does hear our prayers and does answer them—in His own way.

Wherever we go, whatever dangers we encounter, whatever suffering or sorrow we may know, we are in His hands.

While we have the sense of God's abiding presence and enduring love, nothing can harm us—death itself, however it may come, is only the last step upon the road that brings us in the end to Him.

10. ASK YOURSELF FOR A REFERENCE[1]

I like the old story of the woman who, after a careful study of the "character" supplied by a prospective maid, looked up and remarked approvingly:

"That is a very nice character." To which the young woman replied: "I'm glad you like it, ma'am. I wrote it myself."

We could all have very nice "characters" if we wrote them ourselves. But, after all, why not? There would be nearly as much sense in it as there is in the present system.

I have always considered this business of demanding references from servants as too one-sided. And its value as a safeguard is very small. No one who enters another person's household with criminal intentions fails to provide himself—or herself—with excellent references.

Should we demand references from an employee unless we are prepared to give them?

We advertise for a maid, and offer, in addition to wages, "a good home." But girls who apply for the job have to take our description on trust.

We ask them for the names and addresses of their former employers so that we can learn all about them. But we would have ten different kinds of fit if they asked for the name and address of our last maid, so that they might get the "low-down" on us.

Yet that surely would be a fairer way of doing it. Let the employer furnish references as well as the employee.

If we are taking a stranger into our home, and want to be sure that she is the right sort, we are equally strangers to her. Suppose she is a young girl. Isn't she taking a risk in entering a house of which she knows nothing?

---

[1] From *God and My Neighbor,* Cassell and Co., Ltd. (London, 1937).

We want an assurance that she is good-tempered and courteous, because we find it unpleasant to have a girl who is sulky and surly. But hasn't she just as great an interest in learning what sort of temper we have?

All along the line it is the same. There is nothing that we want to know about her that she hasn't just as much need to know about us.

Even if we admit this, we don't like the idea of a girl we're going to employ getting her first mental picture of us from a former maid.

There have been certain little unpleasantnesses—perhaps it is because of one of these that we are changing our domestic staff. So we feel that the "reference" our late employee would give might not be flattering.

Wait a moment, though. What about the reference we gave her? Was it coloured by those same disagreements? We are afraid this former maid might not be just to us. But have we been just to her?

It begins to look as if we can't accept any of those references at face value. They are worthless unless we know the character of the people who wrote them and the circumstances in which they were written.

The truth is that every personal relation—whether it be that of mistress and maid, husband and wife, or parent and child—is a job for two. Each must do his or her part if it is to be a success.

When it is a failure it is no use merely blaming the other person. The chances are that there are just as many faults on our own side. And it's much more profitable to look for those. Only we can put right what is wrong with ourselves.

And if ours is only one side of the relation, it is the side that is our responsibility. Also in tackling it, we may be helping the other side to get right.

There is common sense as well as Christianity in the injunction: "Do unto others as you would that they should do unto you." The way to get the best out of other people is to give them the best that is in us.

This applies in every field of life. And the reverse is just as true.

We can usually rely on seeing the worst of other people if we show them the worst of ourselves.

So there is something self-revealing in our estimates of our fellow men. These estimates depend always on how they behave to us. And how they behave to us is often as much our doing as theirs.

When I find a man with a low opinion of human nature I don't ask what other people have done to him. I wonder what he has done to them.

On the other hand, the man who is decent and kindly will tell you that other people are, for the most part, the same. That is his experience. He helps them to be so.

Here's an exercise that might do us all good. Let's do what the young woman did in the story and write our own "character." Only let's do it, not to impress some one else with our value, but to get at the truth about ourselves.

What shall we say? Honest, truthful, hard-working?

Are we always honest? Or do we sometimes ignore the odd coppers when we're paying a tradesman's bill, or keep him waiting for his money, or fail to point out a mistake that is in our favour, or forget to pay excess fare if we travel with the wrong railway ticket?

Truthful? Do we tell the truth when it's unpleasant to ourselves, or only when it's unpleasant to some one else?

Hard-working? Do we put our backs into it just as hard when the chief is looking the other way as we do when he's watching? Aren't there times when we "ca' canny"?

No doubt there are reasons for it. We aren't feeling up to the mark, or the atmosphere is wrong. But other people about whose work we grumble have exactly the same excuses to offer.

Are we easy to get on with? If we find other people difficult we may take it for granted that we are difficult ourselves.

So we may go on, asking all the questions about ourselves that we would ask about any one we meant to employ. Perhaps when we have finished we will be a little more charitable next time we sit in judgment on other people.

Or, better still, we will decide to take ourselves in hand. We can always get rid of a maid who is unsatisfactory—but we can't get rid of ourselves. And our happiness depends far more upon ourselves—upon our own character and temperament—than it does upon any one else.

So let's stop thinking about other people's short-comings and tackle our own. We're more likely to get results that way.

11. SLAY YOUR DRAGON[1]

Englishmen don't make much fuss about their patron saint. April 23, indeed, is as much Shakespeare's day as St. George's.

There is no one who thus shares the honours with St. Andrew, or St. David, or St. Patrick. But we are, quietly, just as proud of our saint as any Scot, or Welshman, or Irishman is of his.

And why shouldn't we be? He is a fine, romantic figure—this martyr for his faith who slew the dragon. Naturally, we refuse to believe that malicious story of Gibbon's, which makes him a mere seller of bacon, however appropriate such a patron saint might be to a "nation of shopkeepers."

Of course, Napoleon misjudged us. We English are "romantics" at heart. We may spend our working life selling groceries behind a counter, or totting up figures in a ledger.

It doesn't matter. We have daydreams of tropic seas and Arctic wastes. We also would go out and slay dragons, if only we could get the chance.

Alas, there are no more dragons.

Aren't there?

There are, perhaps, no creatures exactly like those on the gold coins we don't see any longer nowadays. Nevertheless, our modern world contains a good many dragons—bigger, fiercer, harder to kill than the one which St. George overthrew.

The fight against dragons is, indeed, a never-ending one.

You remember the description of the seven-headed monster in the Revelation of St. John the Divine, and how "Michael and his angels fought against the dragon, and the dragon fought and his angels."

You remember how, in the *Pilgrim's Progress,* Christian met Apol-

---
[1] From *God and My Neighbor,* Cassell and Co., Ltd. (London, 1937).

lyon in the Valley of Humiliation. There was a good deal of the dragon about Apollyon.

"The monster," says Bunyan, "was hideous to behold; he was clothed with scales like a fish and they are his pride; he had wings like a dragon, feet like a bear, and out of his belly came fire and smoke; and his mouth was as the mouth of a lion."

There are differences, but in essence Apollyon is the dragon of Revelation, and the dragon of St. George—and our own particular dragon, which we are called upon to deal with. The battle against dragons is the battle against evil.

It is a battle to which we are called.

Centuries ago, when our ancestors faced desperate odds, their rallying cry was "St. George for Merrie England!" Among the dragons we must tackle are those which have turned "Merrie England" into a place of suffering and despair for so many.

It is a mockery to talk of "Merrie England" to the men and women of the depressed areas, who have known for so long the sickness of hope deferred. There is no "Merrie England" for them—only the slow starvation of the dole, less adequate to human needs than ever now that bread, the staple food of the poor, has been increased in price.

What are we doing about the dragon of unemployment, which has laid waste the homes of these unfortunate folk?

I am afraid we are doing what the cowards of every age and every land have done with dragons—what the people of Silene did with theirs until St. George came along to deliver them. We are saying:

"Now be a good dragon and stay where you are. We'll give you some of our best men and women to feed on—as many as any reasonable dragon can want—so long as you stay quietly out of sight and leave the rest of us alone."

Surely a great nation, that has chosen St. George as its patron saint, that has at its command all the resources of modern science, can devise a better way than this of dealing with the dragon of unemployment.

Then there are many who have escaped unemployment for the moment, but who are still in the grip of the dragon of poverty.

Think of all the agricultural laborers who are trying to bring up a family on thirty shillings or so a week.

Think of all the town workers who believed that a new world was opening to them when they secured a house on a council estate—or perhaps bought a home of their own on mortgage—and now find that they have to cut down on food in order to pay the higher rents or the building society installments.

Again, this is a quiet dragon. As a rule, we don't see him unless we go out to look for him. But he is feeding upon the people just the same.

Is there nothing we can do about him except go on pretending he isn't there?

And there is another dragon—perhaps the most terrible of all—who may now be getting ready to spring upon us. The dragon of war.

Even without taking into account the various lesser dragons most of us could name, there would seem to be a man-sized job waiting for any experienced dragon-killer who liked to apply. But I'm afraid St. Georges are rather rare today. If we want to get rid of our dragons we shall have to tackle them ourselves.

Shall we take a vow on England's day and St. George's—each of us to do what he can for the sake of the land we love?

But if we are to make England the country she might and ought to be, we must face and conquer the dragon within ourselves.

In all of us there is some strain of weakness, some darling sin. We must not forget this personal dragon. It may seem tiny and insignificant, hardly worth bothering about. But it will thwart and hamper us at every turn in our fight against its big brothers.

Here then is a twofold task—dragons without and dragons within to tackle. The struggle will be hard. But it is well worth winning.

12. THE VISION OF A CHURCH OF GOD[1]

(Sheppard's description of his first Sunday as Rector of Saint Martin-in-the-Fields)

"... This is what I saw. I saw a great and splendid church standing in the greatest square of the greatest city of the world. I stood on the west steps and saw what this church would be to the life of the people. There passed me, into its warm inside, hundreds and hundreds of all sorts of people, going up to the temple of their Lord with all their difficulties, trials and sorrows. I saw it full of people, dropping in at all hours of the day and night. It was never dark, it was lighted all night and all day, and often tired bits of humanity swept in. And I said to them as they passed: 'Where are you going?' And they said only one thing: 'This is our home. This is where we are going to learn of the love of Jesus Christ. This is the Altar of our Lord, where all our peace lies. This is St. Martin's.'

"And as I stood there on the west steps of the church there was a sort of voice—not of any special person—singing one song, and the song was something like this:

"'You that have seen the world and its glory change and grow old, you that have come to the end of your story, you that are weary of pain and pleasure, come in, come in.'

"It was all reverent and all full of love (and everyone seemed glad to see me just because I was poor) and they never pushed me behind a pillar because I was poor. And day by day they told me the dear Lord's Supper was there on His Altar waiting to be given. They spoke to me of two words only, one was the word 'home' and the other was 'love.' I saw, above all, little groups of faithful people whom the

[1] From *Dick Sheppard and St. Martin's*, by R. J. Northcott, Longmans Green & Co. (London, 1937).

world would not take much account of, but it was their prayers, and their service, and their love, and their self-sacrifice which really made it what it was—so wonderful a home.

"And I left that wonderful church then, and I looked again on the thousand thousand that streamed by, and I recognized that into them were going all the great flood of those who loved their Lord; they were mixing with the crowd and telling them: 'We know the Lord and love the Lord.' And there was a wondrous peace and joy . . ."

13. A PASTOR LOOKS AT HIS PARISH[1]

(Record of a night exploring the neighborhood of Saint Martin-in-the-Fields before he became the Vicar)

A much more cheerful experience was a night spent, in mufti, wandering from place to place in the parish and neighborhood. I went into many a strange building until then unknown to me, and talked to all who would talk to me. I was in a Casualty Ward at Charing Cross Hospital, without being a casualty, and the courts of Bedfordbury, as well as several public houses, for the first time; and, thinking in those days that the Embankment was in the parish, I spent several hours on its benches, ending up in the early morning at a coffee stall close to the Church.

I had always loved the stir and bustle of Central London, but it was this night's impressions that persuaded me that no square mile could provide a more thrilling and adventurous pitch for a parson's job, if only . . .

I shall always remember, after my cup of coffee and bun, sitting on the parapet near the National Gallery as dawn broke, and feeling the haunting stillness of that one quarter of an hour in the whole twenty-four, when, as if by magic, Trafalgar Square empties and becomes completely still and silent. When at the Vicarage, I loved to be awake at that hour and to go to my window and look across the Square, for it seemed to me that it was then, in the stillness, more than at any other time, that the needs and longings of those who lived in the shadow of the Church could, so to speak, be held up before God.

---

[1] From *H. R. L. Sheppard*, by R. Ellis Roberts, John Murray (London, 1942).

14. IMPATIENCE MAY ALSO BE A VIRTUE[1]

For fifteen years now, I have been growing increasingly disturbed at the condition of Institutional Religion, but except for occasional outbursts from the pulpit of St. Martin-in-the-Fields I have held my peace; for while I thought I knew what was wrong, I did not know how it could be remedied. There is nothing easier than to find fault with the Churches, but the gain to truth by the mere announcement of a famine is not considerable. It so happens that for the last three years circumstances which have compelled me to relinquish active work have given me opportunity for thought and study, which the ceaseless round of parochial cares necessarily denied. I have spent that time in one long attempt to make my criticisms constructive, and to think how those things that seem amiss and even deplorable in organized Christianity, and especially the paralyzing unreality of much of its presentation, might conceivably be remedied. I think I can see the way round a number of corners that once defeated me. I am compelled, with the greatest reluctance, to believe that the Churches have corporately so misunderstood the message of their Founder, and so mishandled and mislaid His values—the values of his Father-God —that what survives and does duty nowadays, through the Churches, as Christianity is a caricature of what Christ intended. The Churches need much more than patchwork repair.

There must needs be a Christian Society founded on the revelation of Jesus Christ; but if that Society is to be according to the mind of Christ, I fancy it will have to be so wholly different in breadth and outlook from any Church that exists today, as to be scarcely recognizable as belonging to the family of Churches as we now know them.

[1] From *The Impatience of a Parson*, Harper & Brothers (New York, 1927).

An immense revolution is inevitable if the common people are again to hear Christ gladly.

I am convinced that the world is looking for a fresher, truer and larger version of the religion of Jesus Christ, and that it is justified in requiring it. Those who come back from foreign parts tell us that the peoples of the East are wanting Christ, but that they have no desire for Church systems. We accept their opinion but fail to realize that this attitude is also typical of the West. Men, today, are not looking for a religious system and yet the soul of the world, consciously or unconsciously, is crying for the Christ. This does not mean that the world of our day is ready to accept Christianity. I am under no delusion that it can be made acceptable to all. Originally, when it was perfectly presented, "many went back and walked no more with him." I have no faith in the existence of that great crowd which some genial optimists encourage us to believe is only waiting to give its enthusiasm to Christianity until certain ecclesiastical reforms have been brought about.

If the Churches tomorrow were to become out-and-out Christian and if all their ministers were to prophesy—that is, to speak the flaming Word of God in the hearing of the people—it is more than likely that places of worship would be emptier than they are today, and it is certain that a goodly number of the prophets would be stoned. We do not like prophets until they are dead, and even then while we commemorate them in stone and stereotype their message for all time in a form which they themselves would especially deprecate, we should be gravely disturbed if—as Mr. Bernard Shaw reminds us in his inspired "St. Joan"—they contemplated returning to continue their tiresome habit of saying uncomfortable things.

I do not know, and it is not my business to know, what response would ensue if Christianity were set out before men in all its original freshness. God alone knows what the answer would be. This however I do know, there would no longer be any opposition to it arising from the finer elements in human nature which, at the moment, is so distressing a factor in the world's attitude toward organic Christianity. That would be immensely to the good.

The truth is that Christendom refuses to take Jesus Christ seriously. It is devoted to Him, but it does not know what to do with Him and it does not believe that a religion founded upon His Father-God and His standards could meet the practical demands of this very complicated world. It is not thought possible for a religion to prevail which refuses to arm itself with the weapons that this world both advocates and uses. Christendom has acted and is acting as if Jesus Christ had given in to the use of magic, force and superstitious fear, which, as a matter of fact, in His Temptation He definitely rejected as being incompatible with His Kingdom of God. Overcritical as it may sound, I am forced to believe that Christendom today is profoundly ignorant of the very essentials of its faith: Christian people do not yet know to what their faith commits them. The Christianity of the Churches has become an immensely complicated affair and, in consequence, men escape gladly or sorrowfully from its appeal. A new and very real sacrifice on the part of every Church will be needed before the full Gospel can be preached to this generation.

The sense of urgency under which I have written has, I fear, caused me to be less than generous and possibly less than just in acknowledging the inestimable service that Institutional Religion has rendered and is rendering to humanity at large and to individuals in particular. One thing I may be permitted to say on behalf of myself: I have made no suggestion in this book that would take away from any single soul any Church privilege which, at the moment, he values and esteems: my concern has been rather to suggest how those privileges may become more generally available.

In spite of appearances, I am not really unmindful of how impoverished would have been our world had it not been for the age-long witness of organic Christianity to many of the things that belong to Jesus Christ, nor am I unconscious of how much that is beautiful, gracious, romantic and true in life today would cease to be if the Churches refrained from their ministrations and active beneficence.

There is indeed a sense in which the Church—"the whole congregation of faithful people dispersed throughout the world," to use the charitable definition in the Bidding Prayer—may yet be spoken of as it was many years ago by the author of *Ecce Homo* (a book that still abundantly repays attention), as "the moral university of the world, not merely the greatest but the only great school of virtue existing."

For any injustice of which I am guilty or appear to be guilty I sincerely apologize, and yet I plead that there is some excuse for counting it scarcely worth while to pause to praise at length what is good now in Institutional Religion since it is so obviously and so disastrously not nearly good enough. I feel that Western civilization will go up in the smoke of another World War long before Christianity, moving at its present pace, takes possession: it is horrible to think that some who read these pages may themselves be the victims of the next war. As I see things, it is a close race now between Christianity and Catastrophe, and the issue will be decided within the lifetime of many of my readers. I am haunted by the vision of what the Gospel of Jesus Christ has within its power to do for a world heading for disaster; while, in depressing contrast, I am sensitive to the spectacle of what it is actually achieving with its number of mutually isolated if not antagonistic Churches, entrenched against each other and each offering but a partial version of the saving wisdom of Christ.

It seems to me impertinent to suggest that the conscious or unconscious need of mankind for all that our Lord amply and generously desires to supply is to be answered effectively by the offer to men of one or another of these imperfect editions. He who feels passionately on the subject and writes about it may perhaps be pardoned if he decides to dispense with the counsel consistently recommended to reformers, that it is more politic and less liable to antagonize, if criticism even of a constructive character be prefaced by saying how splendid everything is at the moment and always has been.

I have endeavored to write without undue confidence, for indeed "I count not myself yet to have apprehended," and yet I have, so to speak, laid all my cards on the table. Doubtless many will deplore the weakness of my hand, counting an unreasonable impatience its only long suit. It is true that I do not hesitate to express and counsel impatience, but I cannot allow that it is unreasonable and I am convinced that it is timely.

Some years ago a distinguished head master, now a Bishop, wrote a prayer for a new Movement in the Church of England in which a petition was made—thought by some a little dangerous—that the members of the Movement might know when by impatience (as well as by patience) they might serve best. It was a perfectly reasonable and a highly desirable request, yet seeing how frequently and consistently Authority approves the virtue of patience and censures the impatience of those few "Sons of Thunder" who still remain to organized Christianity, it is scarcely to be suspected that there may be times and seasons when impatience may also be a virtue. Indeed, the distrust and fear of impatience has become an obsession with those who direct the Churches and admonish gatherings of the faithful:

the phrase "more haste less speed" has so gotten into our blood that the slower and more gradual a process the more surely we think it divine. The disaster of this excuse lies in the fact that there is no depth of failure that may not be condoned by calling it to our aid. Progressive reform and no earthquakes is that to which even the bolder spirits in ecclesiastical affairs incline.

The Churches will never earn the right to possess the hearts of the people until to attain a noble objective they make, and gladly make, hazardous acts of faith and sacrifice.

We need to develop what has been called the faculty of acted promptitude and to reduce the inordinate length of time during which we remain *in statu quo* while we weigh the pros and cons, what we call "exploring the situation": it would be more Christian and effective to act as if the "situation" had never arisen. The fever from which the patient is suffering does not abate because the consulting physicians are discussing the case: death may ensue during the process.

I have become convinced that it is the duty of those who have come to think as I do, no longer to exercise patience, but to speak out, not indeed with a blast of defiance or flippancy, but in a humble endeavor to assist where one may. This obligation is not to be denied even to the lowliest working partner in a great concern. Christianity badly needs rash men who will not flinch from the crispness of religion, nor fear the result of stirring up wasps' nests.

There are times in history when decisive and courageous action is the only safe course to pursue; when it is high time that what is said to be desirable but impossible should be done, and done without delay. I am convinced that such a time for Christianity has arrived; that is, if it is to have any hand in persuading humanity to try the better way—God's royal road of love. There is nothing more dangerous than to avoid danger: nothing so annihilating as timidity. There is such persistent and, as I think, unwarranted patience displayed even by those who sincerely desire reform that I cannot believe there is need for one individual to apologize for a show of impatience for which indeed he is unblushingly impenitent.

Why need we be patient if we believe the Holy Spirit presses on the hearts of men? We live in the dispensation of the Spirit, but it is scarcely to be believed, for, though we invoke Him constantly, we consistently ignore His arrival, at least if He bids us forget our unchristian values and denominational loyalties. We prefer to sing the "Veni Creator" yet again, as if we hoped He might come next time with less compromising demands. . . .

Not for one instant do I suggest that my opinions and suggestions should prevail, but I think they should be considered. If what is here advanced is of the truth, encouragement is sought; if false, correction. When by general consent things are not what they might be or what they were intended to be, discontent and the frank expression of concern do not seem to me disloyal though they always appear as treasonable to the contented.

Some who may agree with much that is here advanced will consider that it comes but ill from the pen of an accredited minister of religion who has accepted the emoluments of a Church which he desires to see radically altered, though I should prefer the word enlarged. . . .

Yet I would end with a caution which, with whatever ill success, I have endeavored myself to bear in mind. We who desire radical reform are not called upon to be contemptuous or irreverent to the past, or to underestimate the accumulate wisdom of the centuries. "Modern knowledge," says Canon Oliver Quick, "may compel us to abandon—not without regret—beliefs that were dear to the forefathers of the faith. But before we allow ourselves to part with any legacy which they have bequeathed to us, we must make sure that we appreciate the full value of our heritage." There is a worship of the present no less dangerous than the worship of the past.

If our second duty to the past is to forget it, our first duty is to bear it well in mind. "Each great regenerator and revealer of reality," writes Bishop Gore, "each God-intoxicated soul achieving transcendence owes something to his predecessors and contemporaries. All great spiritual achievement, like all great artistic achievement, however spontaneous it may seem to be, however much the fruit of a personal love and vision, is firmly rooted in the racial past. It fulfills rather than destroys, and unless its true movement toward novelty and fresh levels of pure experience be then balanced by the stability which is given to us by our hoarded traditions and formed habits, it will degenerate into eccentricity and fail of its full effect. Although nothing but firsthand discovery of a response to spiritual values is in the end of any use to us, that discovery and that response are never quite such single-handed affairs as we like to suppose."

During the war an archbishop was seen in a front-line trench in gaiters and a tin hat. Canon Guy Rogers has remarked on the encouragement that could be derived from his Grace's appearance since while his legs were firmly rooted in the past, his head was moving with the times. Of such is the spirit of the true reformer.

15. AN ADVENTURE RATHER THAN AN ORTHODOXY[1]

I am anxious to emphasize with all the force at my command two conclusions at which I have arrived, both of which seem to me of paramount importance. Firstly, I do not believe that a Church can be Christian, Christlike, if it be publicly expressing or upholding judgments, values and traditions—however hallowed by custom—that in doing violence to the spirit of love, unity and peace are alien to the mind of Christ; or which the conscience of an individual, who was endeavoring to live his life so that Jesus Christ could approve it, would repudiate for himself as being less than Christian. In a sentence, *a Church may not be corporately less Christian than the Christian individual.* At the moment there is a grave contrast between the piety of many an individual Christian and the corporate impiety of the Churches.

And secondly, while I recognize the absolute necessity for the Christian Society, I believe that its main purpose and function is to serve and encourage those who have determined within their own souls to dare the Way of Christ, and have started or are starting on that venture. *The Church, however essential, is subsidiary to the adventure of Christian living*—just as to our Lord the Church of His day was subsidiary to the Kingdom of God, that condition of living in which Love prevails. Jesus Christ seemed to want men to find God independently of conventional aids.

The path that leads into the religious haven where we would be, as Dr. Burroughs has said, "is not the path of tradition or authority, but that of enterprising obedience to what the Spirit says in the depths of our surrendered personality." I should wish to hear men and women asked to attempt to live in the Spirit of Christ and then

---
[1] From *The Impatience of a Parson*, Harper & Brothers (New York, 1927).

advised to join themselves to the Institution, provided that it can keep them true, loyal and disciplined in the service of God and their fellow men, and in charity with all other Christians. I regret the usual orthodox appeal which at least seems to suggest that churchmanship and all that is entailed thereby is the first essential for those who would be Christians. Men should be asked first to attempt an adventure rather than to accept an orthodoxy.

I believe that nearly all the troubles of Institutional Religion arise from past and present neglect of these, to me, obvious truths, and that they are responsible both for the fact that the Churches are preaching less than the full Gospel of Jesus Christ, and that the Institution has been given a priority and a pride of place to which it has no right and for which it has no authority. No man can follow two masters, and there are times when it is impossible to be loyal to Christ and the Church. Surely there is no doubt, then, where loyalty should be given. The Son of Man is Lord even of the Church. . . .

In response to this urgent need, I shall suggest that no religion will suffice, or indeed is required for the satisfaction of man's spiritual hunger or the salvation of his world, save the religion of Jesus Christ. One thing, however, is certain: muffled, partial, exclusive and attenuated editions of that religion, such as do duty now for original Christianity, will not meet the case or the need. There is nothing to be said for reduced Christianity.

If the Christian faith be superbly relevant to the actual needs of hard-pressed people, why is the fact not widely known and advertised, and the offer gratefully and gladly accepted? It is here that I shall be compelled to join issue with the religion of the Churches as they now function since I cannot perceive that they are really preaching or practicing Christianity or offering it to mankind. The world's literal need of salvation is not to be satisfied by summonses to denominational loyalties and devotional exercises any more than by a religion of pious sentimentality with its lavish references to "gentle" and "sweet." "At the moment," says Professor Barry, "the Churches are mainly devotional societies." Where the trumpet is expected, the flute will not suffice; and the flute, I fear, is the predominant instrument today in the orchestra of Institutional Religion. As things are Christianity is not given a chance: the Churches seem to have no courage for the fray. Frankly, I desire to see the values of organized

Christianity turned upside down, believing they are now very largely wrong side up.

Yet, a Church of some sort is necessary not only because Jesus Christ seemed to take one for granted, but because He appeared to wish His followers to be associated together in a fellowship. "There is nothing," writes Bishop Gore, "more central to the mind of Christ than that you can only love God in fellowship." Moreover, group organization is a necessity for mankind, and the spiritual needs of the majority will not be catered for without a society, through which men may express their ideals, and from which they may obtain that which they require to keep them strong and steadfast in the way. As long as man is man Churches will be needed for all that moral and spiritual re-enforcement which common life and aims and example and worship and symbolism can give....

Certainly the Christian Institution is essential.

This leads us to the crucial question of the kind of Church which would be acceptable to the Founder of Christianity, and in this connection I shall declare my belief that no Church can be actually Christian that corporately expresses values which differ from the outstanding values of Christ, and which would be repudiated by an individual disciple for his own life and practice as being less than Christlike. Obvious and fundamental as this axiom may appear, it is not one which the churches have attended to in the past; nor are they likely to attend to it in the future without a drastic change of heart and *moral* on the part of the rank and file, as well as the ecclesiastically minded who compose and largely control them. The churches are not societies for the preservation of ancient opinions, but for the furtherance of living religion; they must make and not merely record history.

My contention is that the task now awaiting every Church which will not brook delay is to put itself corporately and ruthlessly under the tuition of Jesus Christ in an atmosphere of unlimited candor, that it may correct its values where they have gone astray, simplify its message where it has become immensely complicated, purify its life and witness where it has suffered from contact with the kingdoms of this world, and dissociate itself from the spirit of exclusiveness and from privileges which separate it from other Churches, and render it incomprehensible to and aloof from ordinary people who have nothing but admiration for the religion of Christ as they find it in His life. This will be no light undertaking. The sharing of the mind of Christ will be almost as difficult as rebirth itself for churches rooted in history and sometimes in those fables that are called history (I am not afraid of history but I *am* afraid of historians!)—steeped in tradition, jealous of prestige, tenacious of their status, confident in the finality of their creeds, anxious for pre-eminence. "To covet the truth is a very distinguished passion," says Santayana. A world of vested interests is not one which welcomes the disruptive forces of candour, but unless the churches will consent at least to reconsider their values, judgments and traditions under a new baptism of the Spirit of Jesus Christ, Christendom cannot be renewed; if they will, then surprising and wonderful things will happen, the results of which no man can now foretell. At the moment Christianity is heavily weighted with ancestral blunders.

I cannot believe that Institutional Religion can be vitalized and made effective for the great task that still awaits it unless individuals who belong to the churches, beginning with the clergy and ministers (for the rank and file are not to be expected to be in advance of their professional teachers) now determine to take Jesus Christ seriously and at His Word, and insist that their particular Church should do likewise.

The problem of the churches is primarily the problem of whether the *morale* of their members can be renewed and heightened sufficiently to compel them first to understand and then to accept for themselves the unedited teaching of Jesus Christ, and later to lay it without compromise upon the conscience of their Christian Church, insisting that its corporate values and judgments should be such as would do no violence to the Father-God of Jesus Christ's revealing. It is no new definition of religion that is needed, but a new realization of it. A new vision of Christianity is infinitely more important than any concrete business operation on the part of ecclesiastical reformers. Vital religious revivals are not concerned with changing men from unbelief to belief, but from mere belief to realization. The early Christians had no creeds and little ritual, but a mighty realization.

The first duty now for those of us who profess and call ourselves Christians and Church people is to rethink our religion in terms of Jesus Christ. It is not very difficult to do this, but to accept the conclusions of that process of rethought and to stand for them is a task warranted to tax every ounce of moral courage that a man may possess. Yet whenever in history Christianity has vitally come to itself, the movement has been associated with somebody's rediscovery of Jesus Christ.

16. CHRISTIANITY OR CATASTROPHE[1]

The great days of religion are those in which it is seen to be indispensable. I believe that such days have arrived and that there never was a moment in history when mankind more fully recognized its need of the saving power of a great and charitable religion. Most people now are willing to confess that a religion of some sort is essential, and it is a significant fact that few public men have any chance of really influencing the masses unless at heart their appeal be spiritual. If anyone has anything better than Christianity to propose, let him shout it from the housetops. He will certainly be listened to.

We do not hesitate to confess that the times are out of joint and the weapons we forged for our safety are broken in our hand. There is considerable confusion in the minds of those who were once our trusted counselors; the ring of confidence is lacking in their speech. The situation is the more difficult since stern reality has forced us to give up our mid-Victorian belief in an automatic progress towards perfection; as a matter of fact, it gave us up in August of 1914, and we have not yet recovered from the shock. We have been obliged in recent years, as Dr. Fosdick has reminded us, to contemplate the bankruptcy of an age which had some right to consider itself the most humanely progressive, the most enlightened and the most secure in all history. We have been reminded lately that during recent years twenty-four thrones have been overthrown, including those of the greatest land empires of the world. During those years we have seen the worst war that has ever taken place, costing over ten million lives; we have experienced the worst famine the world has hitherto known; and the worst pestilence known to man, taking a larger toll of life than the war itself. . . .

---
[1] From *The Impatience of a Parson*, Harper & Brothers (New York, 1927).

We may not forget what has happened to the civilization in which we so trusted. Progress in science and education and an increase of knowledge all round have not fulfilled our hopes for them by making life safer and more agreeable for our fellows; indeed, with selfishness unsubdued, man is as much more dangerous as his power for mischief has increased. Professor Huxley was justified when he said, many years ago, that our highly developed miracles had given us a command over nonhuman nature greater than that once attributed to the magicians. We are not to be trusted with this fresh acquisition of scientific knowledge; we cannot handle it either to the glory of God or for the welfare of mankind.

Now that the ends of the earth have been brought together so that the world has become like a whispering gallery, and gossip goes round the nations almost as quickly as it goes round the village, all that is likely while human nature remains untamed is a magnificent opportunity for a first-rate family quarrel—the worst of all quarrels. Even our higher education has its dangers; there is a sense in which in its purely utilitarian forms it can only do for man what the Devil did for our Lord when he took Him up to the top of a high mountain and tempted Him to make a bid for the kingdoms of this world and the glory thereof.

The progress and discovery of the nineteenth century, from which we hoped so much, have not saved us. Truly our Western civilization is on trial. The ancient races of the East have never admitted the moral superiority of the West; lately they have witnessed the spectacle of those to whom the world at large looks for the realization of Christ's ideals engaged in mutual slaughter. Is it to be wondered that they remain unimpressed when we offer them the blessing of our civilization, or dare to suggest that they should become as we are, and welcome our merchant and our missionary? Have we any right to the assumption that a continuance of a civilization such as we have achieved, based upon force and competition, is essential for the welfare of the world? When the civilization of Rome went down into the dust, no doubt contemporary opinion must have thought that no greater fatality could have happened to the world. Was it justified? I wonder. "The West," cries Gandhi, "has an unshakable belief in force and material welfare, therefore no matter how much it cries for peace and disarmament its ferocity will still cry louder." Are we living in the hectic last phase of a dying order, or may we cling to the hope that it is the darkness which precedes the dawn?

The disease from which the world is suffering is a species of locomotor ataxia—the limbs of the body are working without reference to the spirit. Dean Inge has summed up the situation in a phrase: "It remains to be seen if civilization is to be mended, or must be ended," and he goes on to add, "the times seem ripe for a new birth of religious and spiritual life which may remold society as no less potent force would have the strength to do."

By general consent, some religion that can eat up selfishness must prevail. If we are to contemplate the future undismayed, worldly wisdom and political craft will not suffice. Politicians are not as a rule expert in knowledge of human nature; if they were, they would realize that from a practical point of view alone they could only regain the lost confidence of the peoples by enlisting on the side of the angels.

It would be unfair, however, to suggest that we are influenced merely by considerations of self and race preservation. Man is "incurably religious"; he is, to use the phrase of George Sand, "tormented by divine things." Historically nothing is so persistent as religion, and the greatest of all the allies of religion is the need of God in the human soul. There is nothing so native to man as God. It is the fashion nowadays to speak with anxiety about the future of religion as if there were grave doubts as to whether there were any future for it at all. It is foolish talk. We may well be concerned as to the forms which the religion of the future will take; we may even be apprehensive as to the fate of our own little denomination, but so long as human nature continues, so long will religion, which belongs to the very nerve and tissue of life, persist. Yet a real interest in religion is quite compatible with a total lack of interest in Churches and Church affairs.

Today, men and women are coming to themselves after the insanities of recent years; they are looking back in longing to the lights of the Father's Home where their true life belongs and where the kiss of forgiveness and the peace of fellowship awaits them. In this generation we do not readily use the language of the New Testament. We do not say: "I will arise and go to my father and say unto him"; but, if we meet someone who is trekking homeward from a far country we long for the courage to bear him company. We do not question the wisdom of his choice of road; we merely regret the moral cowardice that dissuades us from a similar pilgrimage. What the churches tell us to think is always a matter for discussion; but what God in the soul of every man tells him to do is too plain for man's misunderstanding. It may be true that the modern man is not worrying about his sins, yet I fancy he is frequently worried about his own moral futility and strange inability to carry through the good resolutions of the night before—surely much the same thing.

I do not think that many who have passed through the severe moral strain that the events of recent years have imposed, have emerged with a greater confidence in themselves and their own unaided efforts after betterment. Few can have an unbounded respect for their own character, or believe that there can be any Utopia for the sons of men unless the problem of the character of the individual, their own included, be tackled. There is scarce a soul who does not know that the only reason why we do not follow the advice of Jesus Christ is that we are afraid to. Sin is not the creation of some cold-blooded and anemic professor of theology, but a plain, honest fact which any man may know and recognize, since he will find one of its main citadels within his own heart. The late Lord Morley once wrote of "that horrid burden and impediment upon the soul which the Churches call sin, and which by whatever name you call it is a real catastrophe in the moral nature of man." The truth is that the world is as it is because individually we are as we are. There are, alas, so many people just like ourselves—no better and no worse.

Yet there never existed a greater number of better intentioned people. We may not achieve much, but we mean extremely well. Indeed the contrast between our good intentions and our very mediocre achievements is as remarkable as it is pathetic. Of propaganda on behalf of good causes there is literally no end: the world is strewn with the literature of idealism, and we are perfectly prepared to give at least lip service to many admirable ideas for social and moral amelioration; but, as George Eliot said, "ideas are poor things until they become incarnate." The present world does not provide the first instance of an intellectual and moral awakening which has produced propaganda but little else.

It is we, as individuals, who are primarily the disappointing factor in the situation. Fortunately, we are increasingly aware of our ineffectiveness. We need and we know that we need the re-enforcement of some power from without which will not merely censure our moral impotence, but enable us to expel the coward and enthrone the hero that is in the heart of every man; we need something, Someone, who can deal with this gradual paralysis of moral effort which spasmodic resolutions of amendment seem so powerless to check. We need the God of Jesus Christ and His power and His goodness; yet to associate with Him entails a loss of caste which few are willing to risk.

Never in history was there a greater opportunity for the Christian religion to make good its claims to turn men's lives upside down and to keep them active and joyous on their Father's business. The world's distractions are frankly attributable to one fact only—there are not enough Christians to go round, and the measure of the Church's failure is its inability to turn out a sufficiency of Christ-like men and women. The Christian creed can only vindicate itself by the production of Christian character. It is still true that the whole creation groaneth and travaileth in pain together until now, waiting for the revelation of the sons of God.

Surely an impartial observer who could read the signs of the times and hear the brave claims of Institutional Christianity would be disposed to congratulate the Christian Church on having, so to speak, the ball at its feet. Is there a single one of Christ's values of which the world is not in urgent need, and can the Christian Society exist for any other purpose except to commend those values and to apply them to life? It is strange that any Christian today should lack a sense of mission. There never was a more alluring time in which to release the full Gospel of Jesus Christ for the service of mankind. The people are ready for a surprising amount of Christianity if only the leaders could show them the vital heart of the Gospel. I have heard men pity the lot of those of us who are commissioned to preach Christianity: I wonder why? On this side of the grave there is no task more timely or more urgent.

And there are three special reasons among many which would justify our impartial observer in believing that Institutional Religion could solve the present distractions of the world, if only it were true to its ideals. Firstly, Christianity addresses itself to the actual needs of ordinary hard-pressed people; rightly understood it does not create but it solves problems. It does not seek to suggest to men a standard of virtue, alien and foreign to their own real values; nor to impose upon them the moral code of some God who has strange whims and fancies on the subject of morality, and wishes to see His servants engaged upon uncouth and unnatural tricks like performing animals at a circus. The Founder of Christianity, in what are known as the Beatitudes, said that the most blessed people were those whom we, ourselves, know also to be worthy of all praise. His conception of good people, the best people, is as a matter of fact our own. One reason for the superb relevance of Christianity to our conditions and our needs is that it challenges us to be what at our best moments we really desire to be—natural, ourselves. It asks us merely to be true to our own best ideals.

And secondly, Christianity stands or falls by its claim to give ordinary men "power to become." If Jesus Christ cannot make character, He can make nothing else. "Christianity," to quote Dr. Burroughs, "combines the most absolute pessimism about man's unaided powers with an unquenchable optimism as to what—in God's hands—he may become." The religion of Jesus Christ meets men at the stage when, knowing what they ought to do, they find it almost impossible to do it. "It is the call of the perfect to what is imperfect and suffers in the consciousness of its imperfection." Our Lord never said to those who sought His aid: "Be healed," "Take up thy bed and walk," "Go and sin no more," without giving them the power to make His words effectual. He never mocked men by giving them counsel which they were not able to put into practice; having once met Him, they had no need to read a Catechism to discover that they were born again. It was good news and not merely good advice that came from the lips of the Founder of Christianity. And the Christian Church would seem to have the world at its feet since its claim is that it can extend the work of Christ by offering what He offered, that is "the power to become"—surely the paramount need of men and women. "The good that I would, I do not; and the evil that I would not, that I do," might well be the cry of this generation.

And lastly, the greatest of all the assets in the armory of the Christian Church should be the personality upon Whom, ideally, it entirely depends, and from Whom alone is its one great source of strength. What has the Christian religion that other religions do not possess? The answer is quite simple—Jesus Christ. And He has no rival in the hearts of men. It has been said that it would be a fault of taste rather than a blasphemy to bracket His name with others in the list of the world's great heroes. He stands, by almost universal consent, alone. His religion is not a religion of words, but of actions. That is what makes it so infinitely compelling. Christianity is full of actable truths. It is concerned with actions first and only with discussions and definitions later. "The highest cannot be spoken," wrote Goethe; but, as Dr. Jacks has pointed out, the highest can be acted, and in the life and death of Christ the highest is offered to those who have ears to hear and eyes to see. Christianity began, as he reminds us, with a deed that was done. Before the talking began, something worth talking about was furnished. Christ is His own credential; He does not need our little apologetics. Jesus did not live up to His teaching; He lived it. Whenever Christianity is not merely talked about but acted out by an individual, however simply, it is the most powerful thing in the world. . . .

Jesus Christ is what He is, not because of any official status that Christendom has given Him, but because He is what He is—the most real Man Who ever lived. As Mr. Middleton Murry has said: "He Himself stands behind everything that He said; His words speak to us across the centuries with the freshness of the present. It is here that that profound saying is truly verified, 'Speak that I may see Thee.'" It is not merely that never man spake as He spoke, but that never man was as He was. It is not a system but a soul that we find in Christ's teaching. He allures even while He eludes.

And there is this strange phenomenon about Him, that there have been countless people in every period who could give no other explanation for the fact that they had tried to be natural; that it is God's answer to their actual need; that it offers them effective power; or even that it is wholly committed to the Love and values of a God Who is none other than Jesus Christ. What has happened?

17. "THE GALILEAN TOO GREAT"[1]

What has happened to Christianity? How comes it that this liberating, adventurous, straightforward and radiant thing offered, so to speak *ad hoc*, to the actual needs of hard-pressed people, has in these latter days become so strangely misunderstood and consequently so uninviting and apparently innocuous? If the religion of Jesus Christ, with its conditional promise to men and women of "power to become" what at their best moments they sincerely desire to be, is superbly relevant, why is it that the Christian Churches are doing such comparatively poor business? I am not now concerned to criticize in detail the organized expressions of Christianity with which we are familiar, but to suggest some kind of answer to this large and obvious problem.

There is an illuminating sentence in Mr. H. G. Wells's *Outline of History*, which might well have been written for our learning in this connection. "The truth is," writes Mr. Wells, "the Galilean has been too great for our small hearts." I know no words that explain so succinctly the appalling gulf that separates the unedited version of Christ's religion from those official and authorized versions of it which are now in currency. Truly, when every allowance has been made, the difference is sufficiently staggering. Can it be that original Christianity was meant to take its present forms, to develop as it has? Or is it that the Galilean has so far been too great for men's hearts, at least in their group formations? It seems as if the Institution was at once both essential and fatal to Christianity.

It is possible to appreciate certain great episodes in the life of the Christian Society, as well as the incredible difficulties with which the Christian faith has been confronted in its long march through history, but it seems too evident to need proof that little by little the infirmities

---
[1] From *The Impatience of a Parson*, Harper & Brothers (New York, 1927).

of men have reduced the Gospel of Jesus Christ from an adventure in living to the docile acceptance of intellectual and traditional formulas. The Church of the Spirit has always tended to be overwhelmed by the Church of Authority, and in spite of the reforming zeal of the greatest sons of Christianity there has been, in every age, a consistent inability, because of the smallness of men's hearts, to understand the wide charity of the Revelation of Jesus Christ. Church History is indeed deeply disappointing, and largely because of the rarity of Christian charity.

How can any thoughtful student of the life and teaching of Christ honestly believe that many matters now looked upon by the Churches as being of vast importance can be related to the hopes of the Founder of Christianity when He chose those twelve out-and-out sort of men, whom He called "the sent," to preach the Kingdom of God? Without prejudice to the need for a Christian society and a Christian theology, I find it hard to persuade myself that there is any Church today that does not need radically to alter its outlook and its scale of values if it is to count itself as actually Christian. If there can be no distinction between what is Christian and what is Christlike, we must surely confess that when the values of Jesus Christ are compared with the values of the Christian Institution, then something has gone dreadfully astray. Dr. Jacks writes: "Turning to the sources of Christianity in the first three Gospels, we are struck by an immense contrast. There is no money in the purse, no victuals in the wallet, no munition in the magazine, no baggage train, no commissariat, no provision for trench warfare—and no thought of it. We are in the presence of elemental realities more beautiful than Solomon in all his glory, more majestic than the successors of St. Peter in all their pomp. We are in another atmosphere. All this apparatus of defense and apology, of preaching and propaganda, of Church policies and Chapel oppositions—things that have given a form so strangely artificial to our conception of Christianity are here either secondary or absent altogether."

Is it conceivable that Christ could be orthodox within any Church today, or that He could sit at our ecclesiastical gatherings and enter with sympathy into most of the problems which we so love to debate? I fear that if our Lord were to come again, He would be compelled to acknowledge that Institutional Religion had corrected many of His values and forgotten many besides. It is doubtful who would be the more surprised: He at our values, or we at His. The Galilean has been too great for our small hearts—that is exactly the truth. Religion has been imprisoned by its little janitors with their administrative complications.

It is difficult to believe that our Lord ever had any desire to authorize a hierarchy of men to define and curtail the boundaries of His religion, to lord it over their brother men or hedge the Father-God around with rules, regulations and traditions which He never mentioned and most of which he might possibly repudiate with sorrow if not with scorn. "The presuppositions," writes Dr. Inge, "upon which Institutionalism rests that Christ wished to found a hierarchal corporation with a divinely guaranteed monopoly of certain spiritual benefits, and that this corporation was intended to be a universal Caesarean Empire embracing the whole world, are doctrines which I cannot see the slightest reason for believing."

I have endeavored to steep myself in the mind of Christ as He speaks to me and to all men in the Gospels and from the pages of the countless Lives of our Lord that have poured out from the press in recent years, and I find it impossible to think that He could sanction many of our accepted conventions, and especially those which cause Christians to be separated from one another by barriers of intellectual apprehension. At the moment, if a priest of the Church of England gives the Holy Communion to a devout follower of Jesus Christ who is not of his own persuasion, he is in effect told by Authority that while he has doubtless performed a Christian action, he has committed a kind of ecclesiastical foul which must not be done again. Can this spirit be attributed to Jesus Christ, or is it that we have come to care more for the prestige of our own Church and the niceties of "Church order" than for the Spirit of our Lord Himself? That is only one instance amongst many that could be given to show the strange pass to which ecclesiasticism has come.

Our Lord meant to simplify and not to complicate religion; not to perplex but to assist human nature, and above all to set men free; but ever since His time the corporations that have professed to extend His work have decided that His message needed intellectualizing if it was to be preserved and that His offer of freedom needed curtailing, and they have succeeded in doing both, even in the name of Jesus Christ. So the free, adventurous religion called Christianity has been changed to suit the will or the whim of administrators and especially of those who desired to obtain a status for themselves which would enable them, under "the sanction of God," to rule the human heart.

Men have said politely that Christ was wrong in His decision not to use magic, fear and authority in the founding of His Kingdom and they have hastened in every period to correct their Master's mistakes, often placing upon men burdens grievous to be borne, which cannot be identified with the cross of disinterested service and sacrifice which the Master demands and which indeed have prevented many from accepting the true cross. All through the centuries the Institution has quietly repressed the spontaneity and radiance of Christ Himself and has directed mankind, either consciously or unconsciously, to an ever increasing valuation of itself.

Even today we scarcely realize how little Jesus Christ is identified with the Church in the estimation of ordinary people who may not be thought of as turning their backs upon God and goodness. The charity and radiance of Christianity has been torn away from its very soul by those who often sincerely desiring to do God service have been obsessed with the idea, so common to all men of small mental stature, that if freedom be offered to mankind it will necessarily run amok. And now we have got to the stage when it is actually believed by a multitude of people that the only approach to the God of Jesus Christ that may be guaranteed as perfectly safe is the channel of their own particular Christian denomination. Truly God has been created after the likeness of little men.

But it would not be fair to put all the blame on ecclesiastics and the ecclesiastically minded, for the world has played a subtle part in taming the dynamics of original Christianity. "Every spiritual ideal," writes Dr. Inge, "is perverted when the 'world' gets hold of it. The world is very clever; it likes to play with idealism and patronize it; that is the best way to draw its sting. The Florentines flattered Savonarola until they found he meant business, then they burnt him."

Perhaps, too, in every age *La mediocrité fond l' autorité.* "It is the man," says Professor Harnack, "who knows religion only as a usage and an obedience who creates the priest for the purpose of ridding himself of the essential part of the obligations which he feels by loading him with them. He also makes ordinances, for the semi-religious prefer an ordinance to a Gospel." The ever-present temptation to escape from the demands which Jesus Christ originally made and still makes upon the individual have been too great for our small hearts.

Men have felt that Christ was asking more from them than they were willing to give. His Personality has been too alluring and His claim on the human heart too compelling to permit them definitely to reject Him and it; it has been found comparatively easy instead to reduce the severity of His appeal by filtering it through a corporation in which men have a liability indeed, but of a very limited kind.

It has often been the way of the religious-minded to submit quietly to the aggrandizement of the Institution since it has been discovered that a personal communion with God through the mediating influence of a successful Institution is somehow much less fearful and absorbing than that kind of communion in which the isolated human heart hears the Christ saying directly to itself: "Thou art the man," "Follow Me," or "Go and do thou likewise." Even while men hardly realize it, they welcome the Institution because it asks much less of them than the Christ would ask. So those who desire to go at least some of the way with the Founder of Christianity are inclined to escape from too strenuous a journey by sheltering themselves behind the walls of the Institution which is inclined to temper the gale of the Spirit of God. Unhappily the small hearts of men have all too often accepted the mild requests of the Institution as giving them some excuse for escaping from the severe demands of their Lord; they have willingly relegated their freedom and given it into the hands of a group of men who were often only too glad to treat them generously in return for an access of power and status.

As a result, the Christian Institution has tended to become of primary rather than subsidiary importance; it has been changed from something that was meant to be as large as the Love of God and as free as the breath of the Holy Spirit—a movement and not a position —into a something that is supposed to have attained to finality and to which man must give adherence if he desires to escape condemnation. If the world now finds that it does not care for the Christian churches, let it remember the share that it has had in creating what now appears unsatisfactory and unsatisfying.

True Christianity finds room and a welcome both for the institutional and the mystical. The Church of Authority and the Church of the Spirit should be one and the same thing, but it is idle to deny that in practice it is not so. For myself, I believe that the exaggerations and wrong emphases of the Church of Authority are much more dangerous to the welfare of Christianity than the undoubted exaggerations of reaction from authority to experience which today characterize the Church of the Spirit. A shrewd observer has said: "We must look to the mystic rather than the institutional type to give life to the next religious revival."

Speaking generally, men and women nowadays are almost wholly uninterested in the Christian Institution, not merely because they are often selfish and morally rather contemptible, but because it does not reflect Christ, and the values of Christ, and the Love of Christ which is as the Love of God. I have never yet heard any man refused a hearing who preached the strong Christ of the New Testament. Jesus Christ draws all men when He is lifted up—but I have never yet seen any look of deep interest on the faces of an audience when a man, however able, was attempting to make enthusiastic converts to the Institution. To most the Church means nothing but a dreary succession of observances which it is the clergyman's thankless task to exact from a mystified and rather bored congregation once a week. It is thought that some sort of merit attaches to those who will go through with the business, but men do not expect to enjoy it. The Archbishop of York, who knows whereof he speaks, has lately used these words: "While Christ attracts, the Church repels."

Is it not true that while our Lord still allures the hearts of men, the authorized and official Churches do not give them any real impression that they exist to project Him into life, to stand for His values and to renew in His Name the divine offer of human companionable love and the liberating "power to become," which are the things which men long to find in their God and which they instinctively recognize as being supreme in Jesus Christ?

We must face and deal with this terrible, bludgeoning fact that the most thoughtful men today have long ceased to expect redress for the world's distractions from the Christian Churches.

Frankly, it is asked, is the Church Christian—Christlike? Is it standing for the moral values that Jesus Christ proclaimed? Is it offering men the friendship of God and the inexorable freedom of their own spiritual growth? Is it full of the spirit and charity of Jesus Christ? Is He at its center? If not, what is its *raison d'être*?

A Church that does not obviously reflect Christ cannot be spoken of as the Body of Christ. A Church that is inextricably mixed with this world, accepting the world's values, stressing national and denominational enthusiasms, and, as a general rule, preaching a mild religion of "good form"—the religion of an English gentleman with the English underlined—is not being responsive either to Christ or to the needs of this age. Truly, to be a "good Churchman" is often a positive bar to enthusiasm and to the enterprise of faith. No Church can have the right values that puts these things in its programme as paramount and sufficient. "I confess," says a recent writer, "that in some Church services that I have attended I have found myself wondering whether after all they were teaching Christianity, or a kind of English respectability which was not really a religious thing at all." The whole Gospel in reality is summed up in the two words, "Follow Me."

Politicians in their moments of insight tell us that nothing can usefully happen until there is a change of heart in the peoples of the world. They can themselves do little but call upon the Christian leaders to effect that change of heart, and there follows a series of sermons under some such title as "Christ or Chaos." The religious leaders are under the impression that they are offering Christ to the people as an alternative to chaos but, as a matter of fact, they are doing nothing of the sort. They are not so much offering Christ as that particular form of Churchmanship which they themselves affect—a wholly different matter. When will the leaders of Christianity learn that by the judgment of their God and the verdict of men the exclusive spirit and Christianity are for ever incompatible? "We must put out," so it has been said, "on the unknown ocean of completest possible tolerance, not only because Christ ventured so much for the sake of inclusion, but because these vast waters seem to be the only religious sea yet unexplored while all other coasts are littered with the wrecks of the Christian Faith."

And why should men enthuse about the Christian Churches as they now know them? How many find the soul of Christ at the ceremonies of their parish church or local chapel? How many find the spirit of Christ where church people are gathered together in His Name? How many men and women are taught to think of God genially as the divine Lover of men Whose will it is that all men should be saved, and how many in their moments of joy or sorrow ever truly exclaim: "I was glad when they said unto me, We will go into the house of the Lord"?

The Christian Churches have lost the hearts of the people, not because they are preaching Christ and men have determined that they will not listen or attend, but because they have *not* preached the full Gospel of Christ, which even now would run like fire over the face of the earth, had we who profess and call ourselves Christians sufficient faith to go right out for His values, accepting them first for ourselves, and then requiring that our own Church should acclaim them as essential for its corporate life.

As things are now, I do not want to importune any man into this or that Church unless, after a process of thought, he can be brought to see that it will keep him close to his Lord, vigorous in service, and that it will do nothing to make him contemptuous toward those who are following sincerely by another path. I cannot blame the thoughtful who stay without the Christian Church, honestly asserting that as things are now they cannot join any one of the multitude of sects which are offered to them as a full and final edition of Christianity.

I cannot bear to think of the poverty of our present sectional outlooks which make it inevitable that as my children grow up they will be compelled, if they belong to my branch of Christianity, to take up the quarrels of their great-grandfathers, and possibly to question the validity of the route to God which others by His mercy have found direct for themselves. Surely no Christian can have a quarrel with any other Christian; he has no opponents save the world, the flesh and the devil. No longer can I wax enthusiastic about a Church that does not respect and welcome the religious opinions of people of other outlook and upbringing and does not treat their beliefs as reverently as it would wish its own to be treated. I am not pleading here for uniformity of thought and worship but for a number of Churches welcoming, supplementing and rejoicing in one another, and for a mutual toleration of divergent uses within the fellowship of one universal Society whose business it is to unite in confronting anti-Christ. My plea is not for the end of differences between Christians, but only for the recognition of their secondary importance.

And lastly, Christianity is not intellectualism. When all is said there are very few things in the Christian faith that are of vital importance and these are not intellectual. What has all this emphasis on intellectualism to do with the religion of Jesus Christ? . . .

There are too many theologians who are more interested in scoring off the other fellow and keeping the ball rolling than in seeking for the truth; of them individually it might be said as Emil Ludwig has said of Napoleon, "He was always clever, but he never grew wise."

Also, it is high time that some theologians remembered that it is definitely unmoral to declaim: "Thus saith the Lord," when it would be truer to say, "This is my opinion and the opinion of those who think with me."

My concern in this chapter has been to prove what I fear needs very little proof, that if there is but little enthusiasm for Organized Religion and if the Churches are doing comparatively poor business, at least part of the reason is that the full Gospel of Jesus Christ in all its straightforward simplicity is not being preached by the Churches. I know that many will rise up to tell me that this is a selfish age; that men are not prepared for sacrifice; that women are thoughtless and careless, and that high ideals have no hold upon this generation. Be that as it may, when the Christian Church has offered the nation the full Gospel, then it may be true that the nation will refuse it, but until that has come to pass I can neither count men and women blameworthy who are not interested in the partial presentation of Christ which each Church gives, nor can I admit that the Christian Gospel would be preached to this age in vain.

After all, the heroism of our generation is not to be doubted; nor its power and willingness to think things out and through; nor its hatred of sham and humbug; nor its love of what is real and sincere; nor its devotion to the person of Christ.

Maybe it is time that the Churches, following the example of their Master, should die for the people; they have lived for themselves too long. I pray that my Church—which, let me frankly acknowledge, I believe to be the largest-hearted Church in Christendom and which I love dearly, not perhaps as it is but as it might be—and that every other Church should ask of itself this one straightforward question: "If this Church to which I belong is not everywhere assisting men to be what at their best moments they desire to be, that is, followers of the standards of Christ; if it is identified with values that Jesus Christ would not approve and is not identified with Christlikeness; if Christ is not at its centre; if it is uncharitable and crippled by the spirit of exclusiveness; what should be done without delay by way of amendment and by way of sacrifice that the voice of Christ may be heard in all its original freshness, that the power of God may be known and that the attractiveness of unconscious goodness may be brought into its own?"

There is no cause on earth for which one who cares about the future of mankind could better pray and work than for the recovery of vital Christianity. It is never too late to enlarge men's small hearts and their Churches for Christ's sake. We must cease to think that the pains of growth are the pangs of death. Mercifully the Spirit of God is still pressing upon the world; He will enter wherever He sees a desire, however faint, to welcome Him. God cannot withhold His grace; it is we who refuse it. I would not have the effrontery or even take the pains to write this book did I not believe that there is still a great future for Institutional Christianity, if only it would but recite the "Veni Creator" and receive without question, doubt or fear the guidance which He has for these days; not shirking the chaos and confusion which must ensue.

Above all things, it seems to me essential that we of the Christian Churches should now attempt individually to enlarge our hearts by a greater adventure in the art of Christian living, by an increase of thought and constant communication in prayer with Jesus Christ Himself, so that we may be great enough to comprehend the breadth, and length, and depth, and height, and to know the love of Christ, which passeth understanding.

Am I asking for a cheapened Gospel by suggesting that we should no longer lay stress upon many values now thought of as of such paramount importance? I do not think so. Indeed I believe that a simplified religion would cost men much more than this complicated one to which we are so addicted. It is infinitely easier to receive the theology of a Church, to obey its rules and to shout its battlecries than to undertake the awe-ful task of accepting and living out in life the values which Jesus Christ ascribed to God, accepted for Himself, and asks from those who would be His disciples. Yet this and nothing else is Christianity.

18. THE SERMON[1]

(Preached at the Consecration of the Rev. William Temple, D.Litt., Bishop of Manchester, in York Minster, on Tuesday, January 25, 1921, by the Rev. H. R. L. Sheppard.)

II Corinthians 2:16: "And who is sufficient for these things?" or, as Dr. Moffatt translates it, "And who is qualified for this career?"

The Church of Christ exists not merely to record history, but to make it, and it is well that on St. Paul's Day we should be engaged both in commemorating and in making our history.

Years ago, as a layman, I remember writing a letter, which must have been quite extraordinarily beside the mark, to a friend of my father's who was about to become a Bishop. It was a foolish letter—a letter of congratulation such as might have been appropriately posted to some one about to obtain his life's ambition and to enter into an easy and delightful heritage, with some cares, no doubt, but with many more compensations. How little in those days one understood the situation! There came an answer to my letter, a wholly unsatisfactory answer as it seemed to me. It was this: "Please" (and the please was underlined) "do not congratulate, but pray for me." I do not think I did; I was disappointed. The humility seemed just a trifle overdone, but no doubt that was the sort of thing that a new Bishop was expected to say. I had failed, and failed quite dismally, to understand—I understand now and I can imagine how a man who is about to bow his shoulders under the gift of a greater burden of care and responsibility than he has ever carried—a burden that he must bear all his days—must yearn in his soul for the assistance of prayer. It was a not uncommon experience for us in the grave days of war to bid Godspeed to some young knight as he went forth to his great adven

[1] From *St. Martin's Review* (London), February, 1921.

ture. We were glad that he did not hold back. The welfare of our cause depended on such as he being in the forefront of the struggle. He was the best that we could provide. We sped him on his way with hope and even with gladness, but we also kept him in our prayers. We prayed not that he might escape the burden and heat of the day, or be spared the hardest tasks, but that, whatever was laid upon him, he might not fail either in achievement or in hope.

It is impossible for me to exaggerate the magnitude of the struggle that lies now before the Church of Christ if the soul of the world is to be saved. Listen, if you will, for one moment to the sound outside these hallowed walls of a baffled, restless, disillusioned world—at its heart incurably religious—with its cry, unconscious if you like, for just those things which the Church of Christ exists to offer.

Realize for one moment, if you can, how incessant the struggle must be and what strange new chapters of Church history need to be written before men know that we hold the treasure for want of which the world is well-nigh bankrupt, and before Christ shall come into His own again. Think, again, for one moment, if you will, what it will cost to be in the forefront of that struggle and to take a hand in the writing of those new chapters. In God's name, let your vision of the Church's task be as wide as the world—that is, as the love of God—and over against the biggest vision that you can conjure up set the simple picture (for which this great service is but the fit setting) of a man young in years, if old in wisdom and achievement, himself the son of a just and glorious old warrior, drawing away from the comparative peace of quieter paths for the very forefront of the battle, not in confidence, but in humility to take a leader's place when the struggle is fierce, so that no man can yet say whether Christ or his enemies shall triumph. If these two pictures that I have ventured all too poorly to hold before you commend themselves to you as true, then later there shall be a great stillness in this grand old Minster as of men and women at prayer. Even the spectacle and noble ritual of a Consecration Service shall be forgotten while we speed this new Father in God on his way, and pray not that he may escape the burden and heat of the day, or that he may be spared the hardest tasks, but that whatever be laid upon him he by God's grace may not fail either in achievement or in hope. Will you link also with his name in your prayers the name of her who will be by his side, and whose task in its own way will be no less difficult than his?

We shall pray especially for an ever-increasing measure of that one supreme and priceless gift of heaven, which more than anything else sets forth before men the strength and loveliness of Christ—I mean the power to love. It is greater by far than the gift of wisdom or of speech, by itself it is infinitely attractive—linked, as please God it will be in the Diocese of Manchester, with wisdom and ability it may be utterly and completely irresistible. It has its highest source, I believe, in simple daily companying with Jesus of Nazareth, the lover and saviour of men and the master of the craft of actual living. It is captured on the heights for use in the valleys below. It is very lovely, very courteous, very compelling. It can see Christ in the eyes of every man and woman, foe as well as friend. It constrains to silence as often as to speech. It is a lovely, spontaneous thing that cannot always work to plan, but must at times leave the ordered sequence of affairs at the sight of a child's tears or the sound of a woman's sob. He who possesses it does not love the poor and the outcast because he ought to—as all too often philanthropists love their cases with a painstaking professional love that is unlovely even to see—but if he has captured on the heights the love of God he loves because he cannot help loving, he can do nothing else. It is strong this love, strong with the strength of Christ, strong to anger, strong to pity, strong to understand how easy it is to be a sinner, how common it is to be a failure. It cares nothing for the dignity of its position or its office, and so it sometimes dares to step in where it is said that angels would fear to tread, and often in consequence it displeases men, but I wonder if it ever displeases the heart of Our Lord?

Let me end as the mouthpiece of the ordinary Parish Priest—and most of us are, after all, ordinary—what above everything else do we long for in our Bishop? Our position is not always easy; many are worn out with the anxiety that poverty brings, many are conscious (and there is nothing more agonizing) of not being what is called successful, many are longing, and longing in vain, for a change of sphere which might give them fresh hope and rekindled energy; a few have lost hope, but most are plodding faithfully on without a great deal of encouragement. They want—we want—a Father in God, some one really approachable, really human, who will look on us as his main concern, who will encourage us in our moments of despair, who will understand just how hard it is to be a faithful parish priest year in and year out.

We shall not grudge our Bishop for larger affairs even than those of his Diocese. We shall be proud that his gifts are used in solving large public questions and policies of Church and State alike. It is right that this should be—only we shall be most encouraged to make good in our own little part of the world after he has been able to come to us simply, and we have been able to talk with him as a son might talk with a father—as a man might talk with a brother—loved and loving.

It is the strength of loving sympathy and understanding that we desire, not dignity, but love that we long to recognize in our Father in God. Give us that and we shall respond and the Kingdom of God shall go forward. "And who is sufficient for these things?" Under God a wise man with love will not only suffice, but will conquer.

And therefore with hearts that are full of hope we pray that this new Father in God may never fail either in achievement or in love.

19. A SERMON[1]

(Preached before the University of Cambridge on Sunday, May 29, 1921, by H. R. L. Sheppard.)

What has an ordinary parson with no intellectual attainments and with the sad memory of a mispent University career in which Fenners, the racquet court, the A.D.C. and the Pitt played parts wholly disproportionate to their real value, to offer to a congregation such as this?

Only a very little, I fear, and that on the sole condition that he speaks from the level of his own modest experience and does not attempt to engage you upon your heights.

Some years ago I listened to the Romanes lecture delivered by the late President Roosevelt. For the first half hour we heard and heard gladly the simple teaching and wisdom of a man who had studied for years in the rough school of affairs. It was immensely interesting and informing. The intellect of Oxford sat spellbound at the lecturer's feet while he rapped out—like so many pistol shots—flashes of practical counsel and insight hot from his contact with life. The second part of the lecture was disappointing. It was a dissertation on a subject—the mastery of which had necessarily been denied to a man so immersed in public affairs—in which many of the audience were expert and most more than ordinarily well informed. Obviously the lecturer was out of his depth and obviously the intelligence of Oxford was bored.

I am not about to compare myself to President Roosevelt—there is a limit to a man's impertinence—nor to suggest that the intellect of Cambridge could ever sit spellbound at the feet of my modest gift of practical experience, but I am suggesting as a preface which is not meant to be an apology that it is my part and indeed the part of any

---
[1] From *St. Martin's Review* (London), July, 1921.

sensible man—be he scholar or no—to speak only on matters that he knows something about.

There would be considerably less confusion if we were wont to recognize that expert knowledge in certain branches of study or departments of practical experience does not necessarily impart infallibility to all our judgments. I am often reminded of this when I hear the untutored criticism with which some labor orators are accustomed to assail the Universities of Cambridge and Oxford and again when I listen to the amazingly unpractical advice which is offered at times to the laboring classes from these seats of learning.

It is of this tendency to offer inexpert advice in matters of the Christian faith that I desire first to speak.

What easy judgments we are prepared to make on the claims of Jesus Christ to Universal Sovereignty—at the University they are made with especial ease. Is it that we think it is given to all men and women of intelligence to be wise also in spiritual things? I wonder.

For some years I accepted the estimate of Jesus Christ given to me by a layman of vast intelligence in this University. He was so clever and so sure. I was so foolish and so uncertain. It was a considerable time before I awoke to realize that he was as inexpert in the subject on which he loved to dogmatize as I was—let us say—on higher mathematics. The truth is surely this and it needs saying, however simply. No one has a right to counsel either the acceptance or rejection of Jesus Christ until he has been through the school where the things of Christ are studied. That school is not primarily intellectual—theological or ecclesiastical. It is not so much a school as a certain way of life where the art of noble and selfless living is at least attempted in the spirit of Him whom men call Jesus of Nazareth. This is the way of life down which a man must pass if he desire to make a judgment on the fact of Christ. No other schooling will avail. Those to whom the living presence and power of Jesus Christ have become as life itself would, I think, confess that He only began to reveal Himself as more than the master of the art of actual living after some attempt—however humble—had been made to practice the craft of life under His direction in the hope of one day acquiring—for the brethrens' sake—something of His certain touch. He is to be found most surely when people and things are looked at with no thought of personal advantage. He comes across the ages when disinterested service is attempted.

He seldom appears as the conclusion of an argument and never in a life self-centered.

With the memory still haunting me of the easy confidence with which under inexpert advice in this University I was persuaded to pass Him by and of what it cost to attempt to catch Him up again may I humbly beg that no one here or elsewhere shall make a judgment from afar on the things that belong to God.

It is no easy thing to discover even a portion of the truth that God is ready to reveal—on this condition—to the sons of men. It is a difficult and a fearful thing to fall into the hands of the living God. Not for one moment would I suggest that those who have dared the essential schooling will emerge convinced of the things that convince us or on the side of organized Christianity. Many a noble life remains agnostic and puts us to shame by its high virtue. It is not to be expected or even desired that all should tread the Damascus road. Truth is to be met on many roads. A man who has graduated in the essential school must speak the truth as the truth has seemed to come to him. He may affirm—he may deny—but this I would maintain with all my power: If he affirm his affirmation will be infinitely compelling; if he deny his denial will be almost wistfully reluctant—lacking nothing in reverence. It will not jeer or cut or destroy as does the denial of the man who has never dared to put himself and his life—at least sympathetically—within the range of Christian experiment. In neither case is a man offering advice on a subject in which he is inexpert. In both cases the advice is to be listened to with respect.

I plead then that some experiment in Christian living should precede our judgments on the fact of Christ.

And, secondly, may I ask also for a rather fresher conception of the real purpose for which organized Christianity exists. It is not merely among the uneducated that its *raison d'être* is grievously misunderstood.

To numbers of otherwise intelligent people the Church is supposed to consist of the clergy together with a collection of people—not especially virile—who enjoy certain forms of Church Services because they are that way inclined—an admirable institution for preserving the patience of the poor and encouraging the other sex in harmless spiritual exercises. The nerve, the essence, the fire of Christianity is forgotten. Christianity rightly understood is—I would maintain—the one thing of supreme practical importance for the world today. When the historian tells the story of England's soul in the years that immediately followed the Armistice he will surely marvel that no one in high office generally known of men and not under suspect of being professionally religious had the courage to proclaim it from the housetops or will he say the sense to discern it.

For what is Christianity in its organized form or rather what ought it to be save the effectual answer of God to the actual needs of men. As a people we are most of all pathetic because we mean so well and do so badly. There never was more idealism in the air than there is today, but I doubt if there was ever less achievement. Every Armistice Day we re-create twenty-four hours of taut and rather emotional idealism. We seem to be on the heights again. "Now we are ready to go forward again—has it not been a wonderful Armistice Day?" we say. And nothing happens the day after. And why? If we allowed our souls to speak I think they would use the words spoken by a Christian a great many years ago: "The good that I would I do not and the evil that I would not that I do." We are without moral discipline. We can climb but we cannot remain on the top and the summit is also the edge of the precipice.

Organized religion if only it were adequately taught and understood is God's answer to that actual situation. It is an offer to enable all men and women to be day by day what at their best moments they really desire to be—sons and daughters of God, strong, joyful, and disciplined in the realization of the Fatherhood of God and the brotherhood of man. Until we venture to accept that offer for our actual needs in international, national, industrial and family affairs I am persuaded that the world which includes our own country will continue to be jerked from one catastrophe into another. Criticism may be leveled in abundance at organized Christianity as it exists today and much of that criticism is justified, but one thing, I think, may not fairly be said—that in its essence it is unpractical. I think it were better to re-echo the familiar phrase of Mr. Chesterton: "Christianity has not been tried and found wanting, rather it has been found difficult and not tried." The supreme need of the moment is to give it that trial which it has never had since that first little company of white hot Christians turned the world upside down and inside out in the power of the spirit of God.

Full well, alas! I know that the blame for the common misconception of the purpose of Christianity must largely be laid at the doors of those who have misread and mistaught the message of the Gospel. It is as necessary now to teach what God is not interested in as it is to attempt to say what He is interested in—so curiously is God's way as our Lord revealed it—misunderstood.

Men and women, with a passion for humanity, are leaving the Churches not because of what is worst in them but often because of what is best. They cannot believe that a Society content to spend so much time in apparently specializing in irrelevances and protecting its altars against other Christian people can ever be as a fire going before the human race in its march through history. Also they prefer the company of Esau to Jacob.

Yet with all my heart I believe that we still hold the treasure for want of which the world is well nigh bankrupt. Would God it did not seem to men as a treasure hid in a field of professional ecclesiasticism and mild gentility in which they are more and more disinclined to search. It is not so much the Church's machinery as its morale that is weak. Many are finding their passion for humanity more easily satisfied in the hall of Theosophy or the labor meeting than in the Church of England as by law established. It is not altogether their fault. Yet men are "incurably religious." When a life is noble it is haunted by God. It cannot escape Him, it cannot rest until it rest in Him. The Church of Christ humanized, reformed, rekindled, reunited could still satisfy completely the hunger and thirst of men for God and righteousness.

For this it exists. For this practical purpose is the Spirit of God available. For this practical purpose were its sacraments and its ministers ordained. For this is its theology—its mysteries—its discipline, intended. The Church of Christ exists to relate men to God, to claim from them what is due to God and in return to give them the power that they need to get on with the actual and most difficult business of disciplined and sustained moral living.

Forget this and organized Christianity becomes but a coterie of people who are playing a private game for their own satisfaction.

With all my heart I would beseech you to endeavor to understand that the Church of Christ rightly understood is God's amazing answer to this cry of a world perplexed and distracted, "How can I love God with all my heart and mind and soul and my neighbor as myself." And as I end may I be permitted to say one word to some of the younger members of my own Church who are gathered this afternoon in this University Church. It is very easy, my brothers, to criticize the Church—not so easy perhaps as it was a few years ago, but still easy enough. It is more noble, if you believe that in its soul it desires to serve God and the world, to assist it. Will you remember in your hours of confusion that there are numbers of younger men within its ministry—some of the best most mercifully within this University, who during the last five years have wondered if they could in honesty remain as the officers of a Society, so timid and inadequate in this hour of God, so reluctant to alter its methods, so fearful of rethinking and restating its thought, so slow to hush the raucous cries of parties and cliques and shibboleths, so eager to restrain the Boanerges.

It is impossible to describe the agony of fierce thinking through which these men have passed. Yet for the most part they have emerged persuaded—not, I think, by fear of worldly loss—that there is a work for the Church of England to do which can never be done without it, that there is within it the spirit of perpetual Resurrection, because there is also within it the spirit of divine discontent and around it the Everlasting Arms. They now desire to be allowed within the fold of its ministry to be loyal servants while yet remaining impatiently, impetuously, passionately, anxious that it, rekindled, reformed and renewed, may be driven on to its high and practical task by the Spirit—the wind—the gale of God.

And to you who are wistfully wondering whether or not to take office in its ministry may I, one of Cambridge's humblest sons, be permitted to cry—For God's sake come over and help us.

20. THE PARSON'S OPPORTUNITY[1]

I am convinced that, provided only a man can capture for himself the spirit that is needful, there is no more glorious career and no greater channel of service than that which he may offer to God and his fellow men through the Ministry of the Church.

To the man who has sought ordination primarily because of a desire to know God the Father through a greater intimacy with Jesus Christ so that more of His spirit may be released for the world's need, there will never come, without grave moral deterioration, any lasting regret for his decision, but rather, I believe, a growing sense of gladness that he chose the happiest, if the most difficult, of all professions. There will, of course, be hours of depression and painful realization of but the poorest achievement; occasions when the light that once seemed so illuminating is denied; times of intellectual doubt and difficulty for all who insist on remaining in the true sense free thinkers; periods of wondering whether the work is worth while and whether the Church itself is worth preserving. Yet beneath all these passing storms of doubt and thought, there will grow a steady, persistent and ever-deepening belief that, given the right spirit, it is all abundantly worth while.

When the numerous critics of the Church have had their say, there is much to be said on the other side. With all its faults the Church has always stood for Jesus Christ: sometimes falteringly, sometimes fearlessly, it has held up before the eyes of men the historical figure of Jesus Christ. The world knows of Him because of the Church; His name and His life story are more widely known than those of any other man. Men and women do find God through and in the Sacraments of the Society that claims to be of Him.

[1] From *The Human Parson,* Morehouse-Gorham (New York, 1929); John Murray (London, 1924).

The Church has constantly supplied, and is still supplying, the leaders, the ideals and the impulses in all movements for the betterment of life and for freedom.

It does with all its weakness stand for the value of each human life and the significance of the individual—it could not do otherwise when its Founder died for him.

I have seen it for myself when the Church in any particular place or parish has laid all its emphasis on Jesus Christ. It can satisfy; its Bread and Wine do nourish, its fellowship does unite; I know no alternative for offering Jesus Christ to ordinary folk. I know no society which has within it a larger spirit of Resurrection.

I have listened to all that its critics have to say and I agree with half of their criticism, and yet I am more and more convinced that the Church of Jesus Christ does possess the field in which the treasure lies, but alas! the field is to ordinary people as a field of professional ecclesiasticism in which they are very unlikely to wander.

The Church because it is a living thing has unsuspected powers of readjustment without losing its life; its death is not prophesied so easily now as it used to be, at least not by thoughtful people.

Many have tried to kill it; it has looked easy, yet it has been found impossible.

"Sire," said Theodore Beza to the King of Navarre, "it belongs in truth to the Church of God, in the name of which I speak, to receive blows and to give them, but it will please your Majesty to take notice that it is an anvil that has worn out many hammers." That is a profound and, I believe, a spiritual truth, and although in my weakest moments I (possibly like you) have despaired of my Church, yet it is my most passionate belief, when I think and when I read history, that there are no heights to which it might not rise—if only it dared.

For myself I am prouder of nothing than that I am permitted to be a humble official of a Society that might save the soul of the world and bring endless joy to the hearts of mankind.

I know that to some the official actions of clergy who think as I do appear from time to time as disloyal to the letter of the Church's law, while others find it hard to understand how, holding the views we do, we are still content to use official forms which we earnestly desire altered and perform official ceremonies which have very little but good intention to be said for them. For myself I can only say that wherever possible, in and sometimes out of season, I urge the most radical reform of many of the Church's ceremonies and formularies, and beyond that I dare to believe my Master will understand and pardon what seems insincere if He knows that the real purpose of my ministry be to make Him known and loved of men, and to do what I humbly can from within His Society to make it more worthy of His Presence.

This that I claim for myself, trusting in His understanding, I believe would help many a man to be ordained if he can feel as I do and claim the same understanding for himself.

Again, the most exhilarating experience to men in my profession is the ever-increasing proof that what they dared to hope on the eve of their ordination is actually and gloriously true, namely, that Jesus, the Master of the art of life, is indeed the satisfaction of a world of men and women—at heart incurably religious. Year by year this certainty increases. If one may so express it, He never misses fire; He baffles often; He eludes often; He goes on ahead; yet for those who ask and seek, He is not only the Way, but He is with them on the way; we cannot fail to see this if we watch and pray as we must.

It is the lot of men in my profession to be used in the great planning of God. I believe we are allowed to help a little, to encourage a little, to love a great deal. I believe that we can by the very nature of our commission and communion feed the souls and bodies and minds of men to their Lord's satisfaction. I believe that we can enlist men for active service against all that is contrary to the mind of Jesus and hold them faithful in that service.

Finally, I believe that the function of the clergy in this great day is not to dogmatize, but to become themselves pilgrims with all thoughtful men on the road that leads to truth, walking themselves in such light as comes to them from the Cross on which their Master died for truth—and asking for further truth themselves.

Ours is a great life—rather, it may be a great life, but its strength and power depend not on an automatic authority laid upon our heads by episcopal hands, but in our own persistent attempt to know God as men's Father and to capture the spirit of Jesus Christ to this end and for the world's need.

If that spirit can be ours, then we shall be able to make plain to ordinary men and women why we are what we are, and what are the essentials of Christianity. Our profession is unique alike in its opportunities as in the Cross it offers and the joy it brings.

21. INTIMACY WITH JESUS[1]

It has been said, and I fear with a good deal of truth, that religion which once went before the human race as a torch showing it the way in its march through history is fast becoming an ambulance in the rear of progress concerned mainly with picking up the stragglers who have fallen by the way. This, indeed, is a useful and a Christlike work, but it is not merely for this that the Church exists.

One test of morale is the spirit within the Churches themselves. "If things are well with the Churches," says Dr. Cairns, "they will be full of the spirit of life and adventure, of experiment and adaptability." These things are, as a general rule, conspicuously absent, as, too, are others that are equally necessary, fellowship, reality, simplicity and, above all, perhaps the application of consecrated common sense to the Church's services. Men and women have some right to expect in their parish church what can only be described by that hard-worked word "atmosphere." They do not find there an atmosphere as if some great business was on hand. They do not catch hold of what they need to sustain them in the difficult and complicated art of Christian living. They find no real song of praise, no summons to high thinking and adventure.

I am afraid it is not far from the truth to say that all too often the most virile are finding what they have of passion for goodness and humanity more readily satisfied at League of Nations and Labor Meetings, or in the numerous Temples of new thought and theosophy, that would never have been raised had the Church's morale been higher. There is borne in on me the uncomfortable conviction that these people are not leaving the Churches because of what is worst

---

[1] From *The Human Parson*, Morehouse-Gorham (New York, 1929); John Murray (London, 1924).

in them, but because of what is best, because they cannot believe that a Society so cold, so lifeless, so faint-hearted, can ever be as a torch going before the human race to light it in its march through history. They have little use just now for an ambulance. I remember, as if it was yesterday, Father Stanton—of blessed memory—(and those who are likely to follow him in his Catholicism will do well to follow him also in his Evangelical love for souls) almost leaping into his pulpit at S. Alban's, Holborn, and shouting at a vast congregation, "Fire, Fire, Fire!" and then just when a panic was about to begin, he went on, "Everywhere, everywhere except in the Church of England as by law established."

I am well aware that I am giving a rather gloomy view of my beloved Church, but without facing the situation as it actually is, it is impossible to realize the great gulf which, please God, some of us may help to bridge between what might be and what actually is. But at the same time there is another side to the picture. Here and there in cathedral and town and village one stumbles upon the real thing as upon an oasis in the desert. Here you see how wonderful a thing the Church of Christ can be: a neighborhood sweetened by the influence of the Church—a people whose hearts are aflame with the love of God, whose minds are stimulated to larger thought and Christian achievement. Life is actually nobler and cleaner under the shadow of those spires and the men and women who have come to love their Church and its Altar are actually putting a little more into the common stock of life than they are taking out of it. There is a definite religion at work there, though it may not be of the kind the word denotes to Church ears, for it is not limited to one complexion of churchmanship. It is as likely to happen in an Anglo-Catholic Church as it is in an Evangelical (I do not like these words of contrast, which never seem to me fair to either side, but I know no other way of expressing my meaning). It is still more likely to be found where the vicar would rather not be called either High or Low, he has a profound dislike for ecclesiastic labels, so people who don't know what is going forward call him vague, yet there the truths that are strongest and most beautiful on either side are welded into one irresistible appeal.

I have happened, too, on this reality in country villages whose vicars are engaged mostly in kindliness outside the Church. With all the will in the world they do not find it easy to talk naturally about the Master Who inspires them, with the result that they would be called unspiritual by that type of person, all too often earnest communicants, who find it easy to say who is spiritual and who is not.

What is the secret of this Wind of God which comes so often one knows not whence, and goes one knows not whither? It is easy to recognize it, but it is as hard to define it as it is to calculate its power. It is indeed inscrutable, incalculable.

What is the secret? I believe it is progressively revealed, and its power is progressively available, to those who are learning to lay more and more emphasis on Jesus Christ. That to Dr. Glover is the most striking and outstanding fact in history. "For those," he says, "who believe, as we all do at heart, that the World is rational, and that real effects follow real causes, and conversely that behind great movements lie great forces, the fact must weigh enormously that wherever the Christian Church, or a section of it, or a single Christian has put upon Jesus Christ a higher emphasis, above all, where everything has been centered in Jesus Christ, there has been an increase of power for Church, or community or man. Where new value has been found in Jesus Christ, the Church has risen in power, in energy, in appeal, in victory.... On the other hand, where, through a nebulous philosophy, men have minimized Jesus, or where, through some weakness of the human mind, they have sought the aid of others and relegated Jesus Christ to a more distant, even if a higher sphere—where, in short, Christ is not the living center of everything, the value of the Church has declined, its life has waned."

In my judgment, no truer words were ever written. For us who desire a greater intimacy with Christ that we may capture more of His spirit for the World's needs, these words are of the supremest importance. The secret of a life that can be used of God will be sensitiveness to Jesus Christ. An attempted intimacy with Him must precede every other consideration. He will be the center—all else the circumference. Without Him our belief that God is love is by no means axiomatic. With Him there can come that massive faith in God and His goodness upon which His whole life and death were staked.

In these tolerant days there is too great a tendency to sentimentalize the life story of Jesus. He is often presented as one whose especial claim to our consideration lies in a nature that was extraordinarily kind-hearted. It would appear that His tenderness to prostitutes and outcasts was the basis of His claim on the world's attention. We all love that tender, understanding side of the Lord's human nature. What Jesus really did was to change the thought of mankind about God. Since Jesus lived, God has become another Being, and one nearer to man. He has become lovable. All through the centuries Jesus has been interpreting God to man—making the human heart larger, more human and more apt to get hold of God. He is our God. It is a measure of that Spirit we desire, and of that massive faith in the purpose of God to draw all men who are willing to Himself that we desire to capture for the world's need.

This is the reason for our attempted intimacy with Jesus Christ. That intimacy is first of all humanizing—it allows us to understand human nature as we never did before. There comes with it a growing respect for every man and woman such as He had. We begin really to believe in men. As we see our function now it is not always to be teaching, upbraiding, admonishing, but rather listening and learning as the servants of men on their pilgrim way.

There will also come that amazing sensitiveness to man's every need that belonged to the love of Jesus. And we shall get from Him something of His genius for friendship and the instinct of what was essential. We shall know whom our poor human love can help, and what to stress and what need not be stressed, as we stammer out the message that we would give. Ours, too, will be that natural compelling love for the world's failures which made men and women happy in our Master's company even while they most feared His white-hot purity. And there may come to us some of that easy grace and spontaneity of spirit that can come to those who, like Him, have earned the right to speak in a Gethsemane of prayer—hidden from the sight of man.

We shall not discount humor in the Service of God—we shall not use jargon, nor many technical terms, nor tricks of oratory, nor flights of rhetoric, but we shall speak as He did in the dialect of the human heart. And yet at times there will be an echo in our speech of that passionate withering anger that burst from His lips, not when He Himself was insulted, but when the least of these little ones was offended or treated with less than mercy and justice. Only from a heart aflame with human love could such awful anger proceed.

Jesus will have become to us not the conclusion of an argument or a dogma or a legend, but a living abiding Personality nearer than hands or feet. He will be a Man, too—a carpenter—not a being playing at being a carpenter, but an actual carpenter—an expert in the art of actual living.

And all beautiful things will speak of Him as He speaks of God. Birds, trees and flowers, red sunsets. We shall not come to our fullest faith by "the grinding of general laws out of observed instances." Poetry and art and music will supplement our reasoning—instinct will sometimes carry us safely where intelligence is afraid to tread. William de Morgan describes, in a wonderful passage, the effect of a sonata of Beethoven on a man without special musical gifts or knowledge, in an hour of desolation and despair. It convinced him in its own way. It conveyed to him assurance which nothing else could convey, "I have ever since regarded the latter [Beethoven] not so much as a composer as a Revelation." How often have I said to myself after some perfectly convincing phrase of Beethoven, "Of course, if that is so, there can be no occasion to worry." It could not be translated, of course, into vulgar grammar or syntax, but it left no doubt on the point for all that.

If the mystical intuitions that come from art and poetry and music give more power to life, they must be welcomed as being among the things that lead to God. And any new light that comes into the world and is proved to be true, will be of Him, I believe. Again and again, it has been proved that the new science or the new knowledge or the new psychology that made the timid fearful because it seemed "dangerous" to the Gospel of Christ has nothing in it that was not implicit in the spirit of the Jesus of history.

But most easily will He be found in simple people and simple surroundings and homely things, and especially in ordinary bread and ordinary wine, when two or three are gathered together in His name.

And no one can be hopeless, for none was hopeless to Him, and no one can be outside the scope of His tenderest attention. (It is for this reason that I would rather resign my orders than ever refuse the Communion to anyone who was willing and able to say, "Lord, I believe, help Thou mine unbelief.")

We shall not be too interested in high speculations and the arguments of contending schools.

If there be an intimacy maintained between Jesus Christ and us, Religion will become so much simpler than it used to be—so much bigger, but so much more real and universal. Yet all the while the Cross is there, but a Cross inseparable from joy, for as there is no real conflict between Jesus, the Man of Sorrows, and Jesus, the Man of Joy, so there need be none for us between our hours of sorrow and our hours of gladness, for "He who lives more lives than one, more deaths than one, must die." You cannot have the joy without the sorrow. So men who look to Jesus shall find, I believe,

> That one face far from vanish, rather grows
> Or decomposes but to recompose,
> Becomes my universe that feels and knows.

I will never believe that all this is mere sentiment and emotion. It is asking for all that is best and most strenuous in man. Nor can I for one instant accept the criticism that a religion completely grounded on the Person of Jesus, and on Him alone, can be vague or mystically unreal or disloyal to the Society which was instituted solely, so far as I can understand, to maintain a relationship of friendship and service between men and their Lord and Master.

I have tried here, all inadequately, to describe that essential gift which I call the spirit of Christ, which, if a man capture for himself and the world's needs, is as a joy and an offering beyond compare.

If this at heart be their real endeavor, that special urging that sometimes drives men against their will towards ordination, then there are no barriers, intellectual or otherwise, that need hold them back, and there is no limit to what God might not choose to do through them.

If that be so, as it must be so, so long as we can maintain by constant and disciplined thought and prayer, and careful study an intimacy with Jesus which issues in the doing of His will, men will take note of us that we have been with Jesus, and they will have no doubt as to why we are what we are, and what are the essentials for Christian living.

22. HIS VALUES AND OUR VALUES[1]

Laymen expect the clergy to be almost perfect, and they are often bitterly disappointed. They are apt to forget that clergy can only be recruited from laymen.

The most careless layman looks for a very high standard in his parson, partly because he is still laboring under the superstition that the act of ordination removes a man, as if by magic, from temptations which are the lot of ordinary mortals, and partly because he does still believe (consciously or unconsciously) that Christianity can and should ennoble the lives of those who profess it. This latter is, of course, a tribute to our profession. The parson is watched and discussed with the closest attention, much more than he realizes, and often by people whom he least suspects of being interested, since they do not attend church.

If intellectual doubt has slain the faith of hundreds, the moral failure of the clergy to live up to the standard which the layman expects has slain its thousands. The greatest religious difficulty of today is, of course, the unsatisfactory lives of professing Christians. We may well protest that it is little short of monstrous that the cause we stand for should be discounted because of our imperfections. We may point out —with a good deal of truth—how often men use our failings as an excuse for their own continued lethargy. Yet when all is said, it is well to remember the situation as it actually is, and to recognize that the vast majority of those who desire to investigate the claims of Jesus Christ will, as a matter of fact, begin with a very searching investigation of the lives of those whose main business it is to expound those claims. After all, it is not surprising that men who so frequently hear

---

[1] From *The Human Parson*, Morehouse-Gorham (New York, 1929); John Murray (London, 1924).

us declaring that Christianity does work quite extraordinarily well in the affairs of daily life, should look to us for a pretty vigorous practical demonstration. Every day there are those who are being led to or from Jesus Christ by what they discover in the workaday life of His followers and especially of the clergy. In one sense we can never be off duty. We cannot expect to plant the Kingdom of God anywhere unless it has first taken root very firmly in our own individual heart. This is, of course, a platitude, but we must beware of coming to think that what we lack in nobility of character can be atoned for by bustling activity or eloquent speech, or the correctness of our Church views.

"Lord, is it I?" is about the most wholesome inquiry that we can make as we go to break bread with our Lord. It is beyond dispute the business of every parson to transform his own life until—all unconsciously—it is capable of giving out the same kind of music that Jesus made in Galilee and Jerusalem. It is that music which still allures the world even while it fails to understand it. It is because it is so seldom heard that the world remains perplexed and dazed and life goes on songless and unsanctified. In passing, it is a strange thing to reflect that with all our shibboleths and professional jargon—with all the sickly and grotesque portrayal of our Master in so much of our modern speech and art and song—we have never yet succeeded in making Him ridiculous. The bitterest opponent of the Church has neither the inclination nor the opportunity of ridiculing Jesus Christ. We are never abused or laughed at for being like Him. We are discounted because we are so unlike Him.

Jesus, by universal consent, stands alone—unique, in history. Someone has truly said it would be a fault of taste rather than a blasphemy to bracket Him with the other great men of history. . . .

It is beyond dispute the business of any parson to attempt to obtain something of the Master's certain touch on life, and to practice the art of living under His direction. The world will be at the feet of those who are themselves at the feet of Jesus Christ—that is the surest thing I know.

I do not think this will remain as unpractical and mystic as it sounds now if you will bear with me a little longer.

To me, the one thing of supreme importance for men of our profession is, that we should catch the spirit of Jesus Christ. It will be well or ill with the Church of Christ in proportion as we succeed or fail. That spirit moves upon the world—it is available, but not in its fullness without the most careful and disciplined thought and prayer.

It is rather a dangerous thing to believe in God—incredibly wicked and stupid things have been done by men who thought themselves inspired of God. What really matters is the kind of God we believe in. When Mr. Studdert-Kennedy was asked what God was like, he pointed to a Crucifix. He could do no better—that is the Christian's answer. The Christian God is like Jesus Christ. There are very many professing Christians who have yet to learn this. Their God, so it at least appears, is more like Thor, or some Eastern potentate, than Jesus Christ. Alas! many of the services of the Book of Common Prayer contain passages which are untrue in their representation of the character of God, and are definitely un-Christian.

I doubt if anything like half the members of the Church of England, or of any other Christian Church, attempt to think of God and His outlook on men and affairs in terms of Jesus Christ. Our faith says, Jesus=God and God=Jesus, but we have repeated that so often that we have lost sight of its tremendous implications. The Church does not attempt to base its life now on that fundamental of the Christian revelation. Were it to do so, it would shed many of its members, as well as its establishment, but it would conquer the world as easily as that first little company of red-hot Christians conquered the might of Rome. Mr. Chesterton is true—"Christianity has not been tried and found wanting, it has been found difficult and not tried."

The fact that God=Jesus Christ is the great contribution of Christendom to man's agelong search into the character of God. That is the belief we must dare to stake all on—that and no less is Christianity. It is this that is meant to give the Christian his new scale of values, his new outlook on men and affairs.

Yet it is hard beyond words to know God as we would wish, for Jesus Christ is hard to know; He is not to be known—in the sense that we need to know Him—by a mere familiarity with all that the Gospels tell us. They make us eager, but they do not satisfy. They ask us questions as well as answer them.

It is not only by His spoken Word that men come to special intimacy with the Will of God. The "Come to Jesus" of the mission preacher is all too often but an invitation to a partial intimacy. He is not fully known in a mere comfortable reclining on His promises of comfort and consolation in adverse circumstances. Men, too, have brought their own prejudices with them as they sought to know Him, and have only found in Him what they were looking for—a revolutionary, a social reformer, a miracle worker, a physician, a kind-hearted philanthropist, an Oriental potentate, an upholder of the established order, and sometimes, apparently, even the first Anglican clergyman.

We have so often looked to Jesus to see what He was going to do for us, what miracle of mercy or fortune He was about to bestow, and so looking we have not seen. In our search for God as He is known in Jesus Christ, we remain blind until we have forgotten our own needs and hopes and wishes. Mr. Clutton Brock has pointed out in this connection, that if a man goes to listen to Beethoven so that the great composer may do him good—cure his toothache, for instance—he will not hear Beethoven at all. This truth is supremely true about our Lord. We shall not be on the high road to any effective intimacy with Him until we seek Him for Himself. The story of the Syrophoenician woman has much to teach us. She brought her sorrow to our Lord, but, so the story runs, "He answered her not a word." Then she did the one thing possible, "Behold she worshipped." She pressed through His silence into His presence. Later she knew. This is not easy—for most of us it is a big task. It needs all that we have of disinterested and disciplined thought and prayer, and even then, in the evening of life, we shall still know how little we know.

But curiously enough, all the effort is abundantly worth while, and we know it on the day we begin.

Already there is enough light to move by—enough faith to trade with. But it is the whole of Jesus Christ that we seek intimacy with. We want to know Him as He was on the road to Emmaus, as well as in Galilee: as He has been in history and in the experience of men in all ages: as He is today still revealing the mind of God on the sorrows and sins of a world bankrupt through following its own will.

There is one thing, I believe, we shall soon discover—His values are really our values, too. The men He blesses are those we bless, too. His desire for our world and for us are what we—at our best moments —also desire.

He is not, as men so often think, interested in laying down the laws of an arbitrary god who has strange fancies and curious ideas of morality. He wishes to make men natural—not unnatural. He offers an overflowing vitality. More and more, I believe, we shall marvel as we come to see how practical was the teaching of Jesus Christ. We shall find it to be the amazing answer to man's most persistent and practical problem, "How can I, being what I am, become what I know I ought to be? How can I live true to my own deepest and noblest aspirations?"

The Church that is most faithful to its Lord will be mainly concerned in giving with power its Lord's answer; it will be as practical as He was. In such terms it will explain the Third Person of the Trinity—its sacraments and its dogmas. But this discovery presupposes a "coming to Jesus" without any thought of personal advantage. That is the one condition imposed upon those who would create and maintain an intimacy with Him. It is the pure in heart (i.e., the disinterested) who shall see God. It is our main business to see God through Jesus Christ and for His own sake. To me there is a certain quality of life that should issue naturally, spontaneously, through such adventures and through our profession.

In a sentence it will be a life of cross-bearing, but a life also shot through with human interests and the gaiety of a Franciscan joy. It is the part of a great artist to produce his talent without any apparent effort. As one listens to the finished lecturer, or hears the great musician, one's instinct is to think how easy it is. There seems to be no straining—surely anyone could do it! We forget the hours of work and weariness, the periods of ceaseless work and practice that have achieved that finished and effortless perfection. Artists do not speak of the Cross—they call it drudgery. We are proud to call it the Cross. To us it is much greater than drudgery, and equally hard, but much more effective. When we talk of the Cross and cross-bearing and remind ourselves of the place it must always have in our lives, we surely mean a cross that once accepted and embraced, ennobles and creates—not a cross that restricts, cramps and represses. We mean that the Cross, which in one sense is disciplined drudgery, is far more powerful even than the midnight oil of the embryo artist, and its purpose the creation of artists in Christianity—among whom it is our business to be numbered. The Cross, like the Truth, makes us free— free to make the song of our Lord heard in the land. That song will be infinitely human, attractive, compelling and effortless because of its background which men call drudgery, but we call the Cross of man's radiance. If then the disciple can maintain a constant conversation with his Lord, the greatest of all gifts will be inevitably his. It will be as natural to him to love as to breathe.

There is nothing so distressing to watch, or indeed, to receive, as that kind of official love which is sometimes bestowed by the clergy, and more often still by church workers, on their people—and especially on the poor. They seem to have determined that it is part of their professional duty to love, and so they love because they must.

They seem like those who are keeping a resolution, made that morning, that, whether they feel like it or not, the people shall be loved that day, say from half-past two to a quarter past five, and that resolution is being kept against all comers. May we forever be preserved from loving officially. I wonder whether this attitude is responsible for the fact that "dearly beloved brethren" which ought to be very real is so often made a butt, for human official love deceives no one. It wins no answering response—how could it? It is altogether unlovely. It has its own set smile, its own unctuous greeting, its own familiar phrases, it is turned on and off conventionally. It leaves no impression of real love—it rings false.

But love in its highest manifestation is the richest, most persuasive, loveliest, nicest thing that God has to offer—it is the only weapon we need.

It is full of understanding—it knows how easy it is to sin, how difficult to live nobly. It sees with the eyes of those it loves. It never makes quick, harsh judgments. It gets to the heart of a situation as nothing else. It thinks in terms of men and women and children, and never in terms of "hands" or statistics. It prefers to give itself to the individual. It shuns expression on public platforms. It has no ulterior object except to serve. It would gladly lead if it could—it would never drive. It asks nothing for itself, but it is human enough to long for love in return. It knows when to speak and when to be silent, when to be patient and when to be impatient. It is at home with all sorts and conditions of men and women and children, and it makes them laugh, for it has a real vein of humor. It gives and gets a joy in loving. It believes in all men and women. There is no such word as "hopeless" within its vocabulary. It feels; it is sensitive to the moods of all to whom it is given. It is never clumsy, and yet it often steps in where angels fear to tread. Perhaps its greatest characteristic is its power to understand. It anticipates man's needs; it can see a situation sometimes before it occurs; it has an almost superhuman instinct for what ought to be done and how to do it. It knows what is in the heart of man. It is not always declaring itself. Like all creative forces, its best work is done in quietness. It prefers action to speech, it would prefer to visit someone in want to making any oration on fellowship. It likes best to do small things that no one else has seen need doing. It sees sorrow where sorrow is thought to be hidden, and virtue and grandeur where it is least expected. It is for ever on the watch for those who need it. It runs to give itself as the father ran to the prodigal child, not because he pitied, but because he couldn't do without his son. It washes the disciples' feet as He did because it wants to—not because there is a lesson in humility to be taught. It is like a window through which can be heard all the cries of the market place without. It knows no barrier of rank or class, of creed or color. It overflows the boundary of its own denomination—no official channels can hold it entirely. It flows, perhaps, most tenderly to those who never enter church, and care little for the love of God. It sees the crown of their need on their foreheads and longs to be of service.

It is always courteous, especially to women. It knows that He Who is Love had a Mother; it recognizes that, save for the faith and moral courage of women, it would indeed have gone hard with His Cause. It suffers no slighting things to be said of them. It respects them too much. It grieves and is silent when they fail. It is courteous—this Love —to older people and quite young people, too. It likes them to say what they feel. It enters a slum dwelling with as much respect as it enters the lordly mansion. It could not patronize if it tried—it understands too much. It is generous, yet strong in controversy. It seeks to win without wounding—it never descends to personal abuse, or bitter speech. It is sometimes angry, for there is nothing sickly or sentimental about it. It is never shocked. When it is angry it is because another is hurt—in soul, or mind, or body. It knows nothing of jealousy—it rejoices in another's success. It is never petty or mean. It has all things in their right proportion. It is ever seeking to disentangle itself from irrelevancies.

It learns more in listening than in speech. It is never sarcastic, for it knows that by such means no soul was ever won. It is the property of no clique—it wears no ecclesiastical badge.

It cares nothing for its own status—there is nothing professional about it. It is not always trying to buy up the opportunity, to point the lesson, and draw the moral. Above all, its faith in God is massive. It is confident always that in the end darkness must flee before the light.

This love which comes of God through Jesus Christ is the one weapon we need. If we who are to serve in the Society of Christ could possess it from a constant conversation with our Lord, we shall not have lived in vain.

Men who see it will know from whence it comes, and they will give praise to God Who can do such great things. They will also know why we are what we are and what are the essentials of Christianity.

23. ON PREACHING[1]

Sermons are not listened to as gladly as they used to be: now they are tolerated rather than welcomed. It is not because there are no good preachers left. But this is a practical age, and people are very distrustful of moral exhortation: it seems to get so little done. Causes are not now judged by what even their best advocates have to say about them; men think for themselves.

There was a time when the Church was the only educative force in the country, so that the clergy spoke to an illiterate congregation. Today the monopoly of wisdom is by no means confined to the pulpit, and the atmosphere of democracy is in the blood of the new generation. It takes the form of an almost unlimited assertion of the right of private judgment, though it is often forgotten that this unquestioned "right" should be conditioned by the pains that are taken to form the judgment. Nevertheless the claim persists, and it affects men's attitude toward the hearing of sermons.

Religion, too, has become more and more a matter of inward and personal experience. Authority is questioned and distrusted. This was summed up as tersely as possible by the midshipman who wrote from the North Sea: "Our Padre is no damned good, he begins all his sermons with, 'This is the day on which the Church bids us . . .'"

Roughly speaking, the same thing is in the mind of the man in the pew, but if this is remembered, the preacher may still wield an enormous influence for good. There are certain things he does not require, and certain things he cannot do without. He need not, thank God, be an orator; it will be better for his soul's sake if he is not. Although the scholar who can preach simply has a rare power, no

---
[1] From *The Human Parson*, Morehouse-Gorham (New York, 1929); John Murray (London, 1924).

preacher need weight his sermons with profundity, and however much midnight oil he has expended, the sermon should not smack of it. He had much better not work up to periods of heated exuberance, dotting his manuscript beforehand with "*ff*" like the unreal instructions against the last verse of a combative hymn; nor need he resort to histrionic devices of lowered voice or long silences. It would be much better to let any tendency to slang, elaborated humor or shouting be rigorously repressed. He had better not talk down to children, or up to the small minority of his congregation whose intellects are coldly critical. His words are for those who are hard pressed in the difficult business of Christian living. He had better postpone as long as possible the day of preaching without manuscript. Many of the best preachers, who are thought to preach *ex tempore,* read their sermons. He must avoid imitating the style of his favorite preacher. It would, for instance, be quite fatal for Dr. Inge to try and preach like Mr. Studdert-Kennedy. It is not advisable to denounce those who do not attend church in the presence of those who do. It is not necessary to say "Brethren," or "Beloved," or even "My Friends," and it had better be remembered that to begin a sermon with the words "The point of view of the Church has always been" is almost fatal in the hearing of the modern congregation.

The preacher must talk of the things he knows something about and in a language that the people can understand. I do not think that the average member of an ordinary congregation has the faintest idea of the meaning of the words his parson uses. I am certain the stranger has not. There is nothing more needed than a new vocabulary for the pulpit and for Confirmation classes. Some of the old words had better be left unsaid. Most of them need translation, they are as Greek or Latin to simple people, that is, to three-quarters of both the morning and evening congregation. The current pulpit phraseology of religion is bankrupt—by this I mean it is impossible to trade with; I am not denying its worth in the science of theology, but in daily life its purchasing power is almost nil. Curiously enough, it is at its worst in the Salvation Army. I often think that they could change England if they would suffer Mr. Clutton Brock, in collaboration with Mr. Edward Woods, to change their vocabulary. Some preachers seem to be under the impression that those to whom they speak have all had the benefit of a year at Cuddesdon or at least at Knutsford. Great-sounding words and phrases, that have no doubt a noble place in the science of theology, are hurled at the heads, or rather over the heads, of uninstructed people, and often by clergy who have a very imperfect understanding themselves of what they mean.

Let me make myself a little plainer. Words like "Incarnation," "Sanctification," "Justification," "Mediation," and even phrases like "The Blood of the Lamb" or, indeed, the "Holy Ghost," mean no doubt a great deal to those who use them from the pulpit, but they are not understood by the majority of those who are listening. I am not suggesting that these same words and phrases should not be retained where theologians meet together, but that they should be used sparingly in the pulpit, and that even then they should be accompanied with some simple statement as to what they really mean.

An excellent discipline for the "would-be" preacher is to read a work on theology, or the able writings of someone like the late Dr. Illingworth, and then to attempt in his own study to find a language for what he has read which people who were not deeply read in theology would understand. Most theologians who speak and write delight to say they are addressing themselves to a public of ordinary people, whereas, as a matter of fact, they are about as intelligible to those they fondly imagine they are interesting, as Professor Einstein is to me. The man who hopes to give assistance from the pulpit must choose his words from those that are in current use. Nor can a man hope to make his utterances intelligible unless he knows something of the mental condition and attitude of those who will be listening.

All too often, the preachers of the Gospel may know the truth of what they affirm, but they do not know the lives or the thoughts of those to whom they are trying to bring it. Men do not ask for a new gospel, they would be content with the old if only they could listen to it expressed in terms related to their own experience and the meaning of life.

Remember that the religious outlook of most people is largely influenced by the circumstances and conditions of their lives. The Eton boy will accept, even if it does not interest him, the statement that "God is Love," not so the son of a pauper. We must know how the people in the pew are thinking. The preacher must have contact with them before he can speak to them with power. The suggestion is frequently made for colleges of itinerant preachers who would visit parishes and deliver sermons. No doubt the matter of their sermon would be excellent, but good matter is not necessarily effective matter, unless together with its excellence there is also an intimate knowledge of the conditions under which the hearers are living, the problems that confront them, and how those problems can be surmounted. That could hardly be expected from a preacher who arrived on Saturday and left early on Monday morning.

We must know our people. Every man called to the ministry should have as an inevitable part of his training, at least a grounding in practical psychology. There is such a thing in a congregation as an average mentality toward religion. We have, if we can, to raise the average, but we cannot do that unless we begin where people are: we have to speak to that average in a human dialect. When we forget this, we may give a great impression of intelligence, but we shall not really commend our cause because, though many of the congregation would not own it, most of them will really not understand what on earth we are talking about. There are some people who like being mystified, but I do not think it is good to encourage them. Strange and high-sounding language poured out in a torrent is rather like the comfortable sound of rain to a man who is sitting by his own fireside. The torrent will doubtless do good, but it won't affect him, and it is pleasant to listen to. There were many people who did not understand a word of Welsh, who felt a pleasurable glow of excitement when, some years ago, a certain Bishop in his enthusiastic defence of the Welsh Establishment would break into his native language. There was always tumultuous applause, "Magnificent!" people would say, but really it did not help them very much, because for most people the arguments stopped when the Welsh began. It is so with any preacher who strains after effect, and uses language not generally understood. A few will enjoy it, but for all the good achieved, for the lives it ought to have converted, for the Christian tasks it gets done, it simply isn't worth the paper it is written on, or the time it takes to prepare and to deliver. Such speech would not have come from Jesus Christ, Who knew the hearts of men. He knew no jargon of technical terms. He would pass by the grand classical speech of religion which was fast becoming a dead language to the living world, and spoke, with the Father and Mother tongue, the dialect of the human heart.

Men and women are not fired to enthusiasm by being asked to resemble Abraham, or other rugged people in the Old Testament. All sarcasm and bitterness and mere denunciation should be avoided in the pulpit. There is often need for moral indignation, but that is quite distinct. No cutting cynical phrases will help the Kingdom of God, and no man is of Christ who talks slightingly of those who are loyal members of other Christian Churches, or indeed of any who are the adherents of other religions which seem to bring them near to God. One further warning—it is not always either necessary or advisable to end the sermon on your paramount Church interest. There are some who hammer Sunday by Sunday on the same ecclesiastical anvil, small missionary interests, confessions, more frequent communion, family prayers, Church reform, and other kindred subjects. These things are all to be spoken about in their time and in their place, but they are not the necessary conclusion of every sermon.

The chief concern of the preacher should be to declare God; the man who desires to give a live message must himself be alive unto God, and this does not happen on Saturday evening because the parson wants to prepare a sermon for the following day. The process of becoming alive unto God is essential for the preacher, but it has nothing directly to do with the preparation of sermons. The things that keep men alive unto God are their constant looking into the face of Jesus Christ, their disciplined prayer, their careful reading, their life of service. These things are independent of whether we have to preach or not, but it so happens that no man can give a live message unless he himself is alive unto God. The preparation of a sermon is the committing to paper the things about God and His purpose which seem to need emphasis—as the result of the preacher's own research into the things of God and his knowledge of those to whom he is speaking. If the life is devoted and the intelligence encouraged, the message that is needful will come.

We have to be careful not to spend our times of devotion and reading in trying to discover points for sermons. I have known a good many hard-pressed parish clergy who have lost all the benefits that they might have had from a retreat, because they have spent most of the time listening to the addresses with a view to their own sermons for the next Sunday. It is a pity, I always think, that students at theological colleges are encouraged to take notebook and pencil with them to their quiet days: it is liable to start what may become a disastrous habit, as we who still have to fight against it know. In so far as it is true that it is harder to missionize the clergy than any other body of men, it is, I fear, because we have become so accustomed to listening to sermons either for the purpose of criticizing or of repeating them in our own. We have been outside the range of their converting power. Times of devotion and study are for no other purpose than that we should be alive unto God. He who is will be able to declare God through Jesus Christ.

The preacher who will commend our Lord is he who is really simple and genuine, who does not ask for tasks to be done that he does not do himself. He will be alongside of his people, fellow pilgrim with them in the search for truth. He will not think that he has discovered all truth. He will not attempt to pretend that there are no mysteries which have not been revealed to him. He will not be ashamed of admitting that there are problems he cannot answer. It is the belief of most people that no intellectual doubts ever shadow the soul of the parson. "If only I had a faith like yours" is the phrase that is used. Why shouldn't they know by the humility of the clergy's pulpit speaking that they, too, have been again and again in doubt and difficulties, and that they, too, have had periods when, like their Lord, they murmur, "My God, my God, why hast Thou forsaken Me?"

It has come to be believed by many people that it is wrong to doubt, whereas all who have won a living and creative faith in God are bound to go through the Valley of Perplexity. There are many who think there is something wrong with them because they doubt, whereas they are really passing down the way that leads to God. And how much of this conception is due to the cocksure way in which preachers dismiss the largest problems and seem to suggest that God does not approve of intellectual doubt. The attitude of humility that one desires to discover in the preacher is not that of the man who is always apologizing for his own view, but that of a man who gives his views respectfully for what they are worth, and knows that some who hear them know more than he does, if only because they have served longer in the school and workshop of Christ. He will respect his congregation, he will remember that it is not necessary or likely that all should think or feel as he does, or find their faith confirmed as he has found his. He will offer what he has as humbly and respectfully as he can, realizing that his offering would be much larger if he knew the manifold way in which his people were coming to the knowledge of their Saviour, and had their experience as well as his own. He will not suggest that his is a monopoly of wisdom. He will realize that God has many ways of making Himself known to many people. He will avoid that hard unsympathetic insistence on his own path, as being the only way that leads to God. He may be convinced that for him it is the way, and such things as come to him as he treads it may confirm him in his conviction, but he has no right to say, "This only is the road, take this because it is good for me, accept this because it was proved efficacious by the men of the Oxford or the Evangelical Movement, this is what you must do, this is how you must feel, and this is how you must express your feelings, or something is wrong." I would rather be guilty of being a little too vague than of the charge of being a little too definite in matters that pertain to God. It is the part of a preacher to make people think: it is a primary Christian duty.

The parable of the ferment of leaven in a mass of meal is a vivid forecast of our Lord's effect on the minds of men. He found a world of established ideas, and the effect of His coming was a struggle between inheritance and experience. "It was said to them of old times —but I say unto you."

Our Lord would have no quarrel with anyone who struck out a new line or was searching for a new truth. There is no one who rejoices more in the adventurer. "Flesh and blood hath not revealed it unto thee, but My Father which is in heaven," He once said to an exploring mind. The very existence of Jesus, says Dr. Glover, has been to humanity one of the greatest stimulants to thought: and one of the greatest factors in developing the human mind.

Historically, one of the marks of the Early Church was that, though it did not come from the upper ranks of society and had not the highest culture, it mastered the ancient world all along the line. A man awakened to one set of interests is more apt to understand another. The redeemed man is always ahead of what he was before; and the more fully he is remade by Jesus Christ the more he goes ahead. Conquering and to conquer is a true description of the Christian soldier as well as of his leader. Remember, Jesus is the Man Who has stirred mankind to its depths and set the world on fire.

The new preaching, the new evangelization for which the world waits, will, I believe, be concerned with holding up before men God as known in Jesus Christ—just as truth is held up without the need of comment or flattery. Men of certain conditions and men who think will see and acclaim it. We who know Jesus will hold Him before men much in the same rugged simple way as did the Evangelists. It is amazing that in their narrative they neither paid Him compliments nor offered sympathy; they spoke of Him; they told things about Him;

and left it at that—except that later they died for Him. They seemed almost afraid of explaining. They saw the Truth and they may have known that Truth in the end must prevail.

That is how we must preach Christ.

The longer I live the more certain I become that if we can induce the men and women who admire Jesus Christ (and that is practically everyone) to do more than admire—to attempt to live in His spirit, they will come to know God and they will discover that state of Christian orthodoxy into which it will please the Spirit of God to call them.

It may not be the orthodoxy that is ours, but nonetheless it will be that into which God has called them. We need not worry as to whether they make their confession or how often they come to their Communion. Some will and some will not; some will need their Communion often, to others it will be more real occasionally. My point is that these things are not especially our business, though naturally we would try to advise in the case of the young and in the case of others who need our advice.

If I have seemed to neglect the duty of the clergy to preach on large social problems or matters such as the bearing of the problem of unemployment and the like, I have not done so intentionally, but I maintain that if a sermon is filled with the Fatherhood of God and the Spirit of Jesus Christ it will of necessity provide the dynamic which will destroy the greatest sin that stalks the world today—the sin of separation.

Our sermons will not be comforting: how can they be? They will be aflame with the burning passionate love of God—they will be spoken in a natural voice—simply and yet with conviction—and in a language understood by the people.

They will come from our own daily prayer and study and Christian adventure, and they will go—we know not whither. About that we need not worry.

24. "FATHER, FORGIVE THEM"[1]

The tragedy of the Crucifixion begins with as noble a prayer as was ever breathed. The first word spoken from the Cross is the last word in wisdom for the days in which we live. Had we been passing near enough to Calvary to catch that prayer offered by a dying man we should have been obliged to stop and hear more.

We are perfectly capable of recognizing what is Godlike. Here is a morality that has never been surpassed.

Christianity has only one legitimate weapon, though it uses many. It is to conquer the world by loving it and in no other way. The moment its followers begin to take part in the conflict—beloved of Churches and Nations—as to who shall be the greatest they are on the way to the denial of Christ.

Almighty is the word we most frequently attach to God, and by it we suggest to ourselves that God can do whatever He pleases whenever He chooses. Out of that came the passionate question still re-echoing, "Why did not God stop the War?" The power of God, if Jesus Christ is to be believed, is only of that kind which is able to do whatever love can do. Love in the end is unconquerable—all-mighty. You can crucify it, but it will rise again. On Calvary the whole heart of God is seen. He went on loving all the time, especially when it hurt badly.

Were I in the presence of men and women who had never heard of Jesus Christ, I can imagine no greater appeal than to tell them that, when He Whom we call Lord and Master was nailed to a Cross, He began an agony of three hours by asking that those who had nailed Him there might be forgiven—and more, by suggesting to God, Whom He called Father, that there *was* a reason for forgiveness.

---
[1] From *Two Days Before*, The Macmillan Co. (New York, 1924).

"Father, forgive them, for they know not what they do." Men would listen after that. Moral values never wholly forsworn would suggest that this man should be given a hearing.

You will sometimes see a crowd gather round a speaker to hear his first word. If it appeals they will remain for more. We must all feel grateful that the first word we are allowed to repeat as we point the way to Christ crucified is as arresting as this, "Father, forgive them, for they know not what they do." Not in the lecture room, or in the pulpit is forgiveness here preached, but by a man in agony, more cruelly wronged and as dreadfully hurt as any who was ever done to death in France or Belgium or the world over. There was a crown of thorns on His head, nails tearing His flesh, and a crowd of sightseers making sport below. The kiss of Judas must have been smarting still, and, worst of all, there was the agony in His Mother's upturned face. At this moment He preached forgiveness and found a reason why those who hated Him and hurt His Mother might be forgiven.

In all honesty, I cannot see how nations and peoples, professedly Christian, can continue their enmities in the face of this first word spoken by the Ideal to which they aspire and Whose teaching they profess to accept. I think it might be easily proved that in this, as in every respect, Christianity is also common sense.

The Dean of Durham has said that there are certain people we can never forgive. Conceivably that attitude is possible for those who are not prepared to accept the tenets of Christianity. From the lips of a man who daily prays "Forgive us our trespasses, as we forgive them that trespass against us" it is a truly dreadful utterance. It is desperately hard to forgive some people some things, but a Christian exists to attempt what the world considers impossible. Left to ourselves we should much prefer to give a general forgiveness all round, exempting one or two who are really the "limit" as if our dear Lord had prayed, "Father, forgive everybody except Judas and the man who plaited the crown of thorns, and the man who drove in the nails." It is indeed hard to forgive everyone who has trespassed against ours and us; it may take months of praying for a larger measure of love before we can place their names on our list of intercessions, but to determine that it can never, shall never, and ought never to be done, is as disastrous to the soul of a Christian as it is to the world in which he lives.

Perhaps our acutest trouble lies in our refusal to realize how hard it is to be a Christian. We are always asking for crowns and chief seats in the Kingdom without a thought of the crusade that comes first. Comfort and consolation, but no battlefield; that is our demand on our religion. The light-hearted prayer for a front seat up above is so easily tossed up to the Throne of God, but there is a cup first to be drained, and it is often bitter drinking and seldom of our choosing. Christianity does not consist in abstaining from things that no gentleman would think of doing, but in doing things that are unlikely to occur to anyone who is not in touch with the Spirit of Christ.

The sin of separation is perhaps the most harmful of all the mean evils that stalk the world. Many of us keep it alive. We hug our hatreds to our breast, and nourish them while they prey on the hearts of men. The situation is complicated because so often we think we have forgiven—we are proud of our magnanimity—yet we have not forgiven in Christ's sense at all, all the while there is a mental reservation that never again can we be friends; it shall not be the same as it was. We have never discovered any excuse for forgiving our enemies, except that we are so generous.

There is no juggling to be done with our Lord's words about forgiveness. It has got to be of that kind that would desire to share Paradise with a criminal—seventy times seven is the minimum that must be measured to him who has offended. That is difficult; how well I know it. There is one man whom I am struggling hard to forgive, but only in a formal way as yet have I forgiven. I know I cannot be truly a disciple until I have done better than this. Also I know that "He who cannot forgive others breaks the bridge over which he must pass himself." He that hateth his brother is in the darkness and walketh in the darkness, and knoweth not whither he goeth because the darkness hath blinded his eyes. He that loveth not, knoweth not God, for God is Love. He that abideth in love abideth in God and God abideth in him.

And there is a further consideration: I wonder sometimes whether we do not owe more than we realize to those who have hurt us. At least they have warned us of the pain that hatred and cruelty can inflict. The people whom the world accounts criminals have saved many another from crime, because they have heard or read the whole brutal tale of the hell that has been brought to those who love them.

Only lately a man and a woman on the scaffold paid to the community the penalty of their crime—a poem was written about them:

Then came a day:—
Judged and condemned, enduring without hope,—
I heard how, near at hand, two prisoners lay
In separate cells, each waiting for the rope:
Fearful of that whose touch would put away
All griefs and fears.
And helpless I, to aid
Their helpless state,—
Lighten, or lift from them that stroke of fate,—
With heartfelt tears,
For them, poor souls, I prayed,
That them from utter wreck
Some Help might save!

Then to my heart
There came a rending wave:
Across my neck
A sudden rope was flung;
Up went a light,
And I, of land, had sight,—
Where, dark against the sky, two murderers clung,
And in the baffling storm, hand over hand,
Hauled on the line
Which drew my feet to land!

Lord, in Thy Kingdom's day, remember them,
Whate'er they did, who helped me, in my need,
To touch Thy raiment's hem!

Is it far-fetched to suggest that there are reasons for being grateful even to those who by their sin have held up before us the most vivid picture of the last act of hatred?

Well might this great question of Christian forgiveness engage the attention of the statesmen of the world. The Treaty of Versailles has failed, as some said it would at the time, because there was no chair left vacant around the Conference table for the Peacemaker. The darkness of separation has fallen on many of the hopes of universal peace that clutched at the heart of humanity in November of 1918. It is hard for men today not to live in the Saturday which came between Good Friday and Easter morning. Everywhere the nations growl like sullen dogs on fragile chains, there is little trust and no Christian forgiveness. Europe looks as if it needs must regroup itself for another universal massacre. If we have lifted the cloud of our hatred from one nation, it is only to remove it to another. One would have thought that the so-called statesmen of the world would have come to realize by now that there can be no hope until each nation takes more than its own self-interest to the Council Chamber, until, indeed, it is willing to forgive with that full forgiveness that brings comradeship and the confidence and laughter that a friend shares with a friend. It is hard to see how the clouds can ever be dispelled until humanity stands bareheaded beneath the Cross of its Redeemer and hears Him cry, "Father, forgive them for they know not what they do."

It is hard for us to make that prayer our own, for the nails are still piercing hands that are human, and the sweat of agony is still moist on men's brows; suffering, loneliness and poverty do not make easily for forgiveness. It is not a prayer that is likely to be said with eyes looking across the Channel, the North Sea, or to where men and women live in indulgence and ostentation, while half the world is in want, unless it is preceded by a prayer for a larger measure of the love that was in Jesus Christ. It is harder still, maybe, to re-echo the first cry from the Cross while we think of some of those who live close to our daily life who have hurt us, only we cannot bring any gift to the Cross, or to the Altar on Easter Day, unless we first be reconciled to our brother.

"Father, forgive them, for they know not what they do." They did not really—they did not mean to crucify actually; they meant to hurt but not so successfully. In a sense, like the Roman soldiers, they were only doing what they were told to do. The whisper went round that we were going to strike and they struck first. Perhaps, even, they thought they were doing God's Will; it would not be the first time that man has hitched his own ambitions to the car of some kind of Jehovah, and imagined he was following God's Will.

Take the case of a friend and neighbor from whom we have long since parted company—after all it may be that the act that brought about the separation has long since been regretted. Little we know the full story of the worry and provocation that lay behind it. It was done in a moment of heat and anger and at a time when nerves were strained beyond endurance. It was never meant to wound and cut down the years like this; also, it does take two to make a quarrel, and even our best friend would be obliged to admit that at times we are dreadfully difficult and irritating. If we and they could see in one ghastly nightmare of reality the poison that spreads from a wrong that is unforgotten and unforgiven we should not think it weak and feeble to speak from our side the first word of forgiveness. It were better to accept an unfair share of the blame than to suffer the sin of separation to continue.

It was a weak thing before our Lord's day to forgive an enemy, and foolishly weak to allow that there had ever been circumstances that could excuse his offense. The world has not changed very much since His day, and the rate of its progress in peace-making compels us to believe that there is room for a little company who will try and take their Lord and Master seriously. God's fools let us call them, if we wish. We shall go on bumping from one catastrophe to another until Christ's Royal Way of loving men into penitence is attempted, and His way suggests that those who have been injured, cruelly and unjustly injured, should make the effort to forget their own wounds—their own offended dignity—their own loss of status and prestige, and should pray for those who have hurt them as they hope Christ will pray for them, "Father, forgive them, for they know not what they do."

25. "I THIRST"[1]

I dare not say much about physical pain. I understand so little about it. I have had my small share of suffering, and I am sure it has never done the part of me that counts any harm, but to see others in pain has been a dreadful trial to faith. I know nothing quite so intolerable as to stand by some loved one and to feel impotent to heal, either by prayer or by physic. I think that our prayers about the physical suffering of our friends are often ill-advised. It were better, I think, to spend more time praying not for an end of their pain, but for strength for them to bear it nobly.

Jesus suffered the agonies of physical pain, and more than that, He was not ashamed to call upon someone to alleviate the suffering. I always look on the doctor and the nurse with the Spirit of Christ in their hearts, as the most powerful representatives of Christ. I have seen His Spirit more plainly in the sickroom than anywhere else, and of all the noblest people on God's earth, there are none more noble than those who bear their pain with consistent courage.

On the Cross Jesus suffered, and He said so. "I thirst." "Now there was set a vessel full of vinegar, and they filled a sponge with vinegar, and put it upon hyssop, and put it to his mouth." In those days it was a sign of weakness to confess to pain, and there are some today who deny its existence. But pain as a matter of actual fact is as real as sin. Since it hurts us horribly, Jesus was not likely to avoid a similar suffering. Only with Him it came last. It was the last thing to be thought about. When everything was done, the crucifiers forgiven, the poor criminal remembered, the Mother cared for, then the Son of Man said quietly—"I thirst."

The Savior of the world was no ascetic, no dream-haunted absentee

---

[1] From *Two Days Before,* The Macmillan Co. (New York, 1924).

from paths that we poor folk must tread. He passed our way and found it rougher than we do. His lesson is, not how to die, but how to live that death may be but the gate that opens into a fuller life. Hunger and thirst had been His portion when the Son of Man had not where to lay His head. Only these things were not suffered to hold Him back from the Father's business. He took them in His stride, but owned that they hurt. He never went round His trials, but through them, and there is all the difference in the world between the two methods of meeting suffering. When He suffered and said that He suffered, He did not pray for miraculous deliverance, but out of the grandeur of His own soul, and with the assistance of a friend, He dealt with the lesser evil of pain that had come to Him as He pursued the Father's way.

I remember a sergeant in France, as noble a Christian as I ever met, stopping for a moment in the front line of trenches to have his hand bandaged before he went on again. There was time for a joke while the bandage was being wound round his broken hand. I remember at the time, in the confused way in which we thought in France, seeing something of what pain meant to our Lord, in this picture of a muddy soldier. "It hurts like hell," but it never once occurred to him that it should hold him back from his purpose.

It is wonderful how often to those who have eyes to see there are human scenes that reflect the diviner ones of the Day of Calvary.

Let me give you another example that has often made me think of Christ. During the War the Oxford Settlement in Bethnal Green was naturally deserted by its workers, who were fighting in France. One man was left who had been there for years, an old Oxford blue and a man of brilliant intellect. He had given up his own fair prospects to be of humble service to his fellow men in East London. He was considerably over fifty, and he found himself almost alone at the Settlement with the work that required over twenty men for its doing. He shouldered the whole burden and soon his eyesight gave in. The doctors told him that one eye must be taken out. With hardly a word to a soul he went to the hospital one Monday morning, had his eye out and was back again at work on Tuesday afternoon. Thus Christ still passes through the world.

Pain is hateful. It is to be alleviated whenever possible, but it is not to be permitted to become the master of life. Man has been taught not in word, but in action, that suffering when it is met by faith and courage does bring to the soul a certain fellowship with the Divine life. There were four lines which Carlyle translated from Goethe and loved to repeat:

> Who never ate his bread in sorrow,
> Who never spent the midnight hours
> Weeping and waiting for the morrow,
> He knows You not, ye Heavenly Powers.

The sufferer knows in the presence of the Crucified that there is an unseen world throbbing with sympathy. The mystery of suffering remains. A disciple of Christ does not suffer less than others. But he is not left paralyzed by despair. He can do something. In the fellowship of the crucified Captain of his salvation he can make the world richer for all he has to endure. There can be more of God in the world because of the pure faith and unwearying patience with which he challenges the darkness.

> Pack up your troubles in your old kit-bag,
> And smile, smile, smile,

is good Christianity as well as common sense. It suggests that suffering shall not be allowed to curtail the carrying through of the adventure for which the bag was packed.

Our Lord's entry through pain into death is the most glorious epic in history. He goes into it with the flags flying, and because of His triumph He has made death different from what it ever was before. Death had once worn the stamp of sin and of God's anger. It had seemed like the entry of a criminal into the dock to receive a sentence untempered by charity and mercy—just, maybe, dreadfully, cruelly just. Here is One that walks through into glory, and the pain of His passage is but a setting of triumph. Service that stops at pain, or that pain can stop, is of little worth. Now no longer can we look on pain as the result of sin, or deride it as not existing. Now no longer can we suffer it to darken our homes, or its recital weary our friends, or its power to thwart the purpose of God.

And one more thought: in His suffering Christ gave an opportunity to one who had possibly helped to nail Him to the Cross to provide the only touch of charity we see in these hours of man's brutality. As once before He lifted the poor woman by the well from the meanness of her life by causing her to satisfy His thirst, so here He weaves into the Gospel story the tale of one rough soldier who knew how to answer the cry of a heart in pain.

In Our Lord's picture of the Day of Judgment one amazing fact stands out: those who are welcomed are but the people who have done those "little nameless, unremembered acts of kindness and of love," as Wordsworth calls them, "that are the best portion of a good man's life." Jesus says these things are decisive. They reveal what is in the heart of man. "Lord, when saw we Thee in hunger, or thirsty, and gave Thee meat or drink? We do not remember it." And the Judge seems to say, "No, you wouldn't. These were things done out of your heart, not acts of charity so much as the forgotten by-products of hearts that were on fire with love—inasmuch as ye have done it unto one of these ye have done it unto Me."

Wherever in the world today can be heard the pathos of that human cry, "I thirst," there is Christ—on the curbstone, in the office, or the home. That cry sounds loud from people who hunger the world over. How the Christ must long to see here one and here another taking up their bed of suffering and walking out towards the cry—not waiting for the angel to come down and trouble the pool. How He must long to see a few more of us step out of the crowd, even though companions think it foolish, and give what we can in answer to the cry of a suffering world, "I thirst."

26. "IT IS FINISHED"[1]

It is hard for us to know the intonation with which these words of the dying Christ were spoken. If they came as the sufferer's sigh of relief, they must also have been the worker's glad cry of achievement. Everything had been done that could be. Man had been offered a sight of God as He really was. For those of us who believe that in seeing Jesus we see God, the Cross is not a coarse framework of bloodstained wood, but the most precious emblem of man's dearest hopes. Set in the background of Easter Day it is the great pledge which we so sorely need, that love is stronger than hate, grace than sin, life than death.

> Though the cause of evil prosper
>   Yet 'tis truth alone is strong,
> Though her portion be the scaffold
>   And upon the throne be wrong—
> Yet that scaffold sways the future,
>   And behind the dim Unknown
> Standeth God within the shadow,
>   Keeping watch above His own.

God came the whole way to let us know that, and the Cross was the noblest and most glorious emblem of a rout that was turned into a victory.

I cannot bear the ordinary Crucifix, especially those turned out by our so-called ecclesiastical art shops, and there is no picture of the Crucifixion that I care to look at save one in the Louvre, where the dear face is hidden in shadow. In Amiens Cathedral there is a very old carving which represents the Figure of Christ; He wears a robe and a royal diadem. His arms are extended as though to embrace the

---
[1] From *Two Days Before,* The Macmillan Co. (New York, 1924).

whole world, but no longer are the hands and feet nailed to the tree. Christ is reigning here and yet reigning from the Cross. It is this Christ from Whose lips I hear the victorious words, "It is finished."

Mr. H. G. Wells says something like this in *God, the Invisible King*.

The symbol of the Crucifixion, the drooping, pain-drenched Figure of Christ . . . these things just jar with our spirit. We little men may well fail and repent, but it is our faith that God does not fail us nor Himself. Our Crucifix, if you must have a Crucifix, would show God with a hand or foot already torn away from its peg, and with eyes not downcast, but resolute against the sky—a face without pain. Pain lost and forgotten in the surpassed glory of the struggle and the inflexible will to live and prevail. . . .

A Christianity which shows for its daily symbol Christ risen and trampling victoriously upon a broken cross would be far more in the spirit of our worship.

The Crucifix on which we so often gaze only tells us half of what has been done for us. It is an insufficient symbol of the Christian faith. The task before those who would portray Christ is to show Him reigning because of the Cross. What was once the dark instrument of death that cast its shadow on the whole of Calvary now throws its glory over the whole earth to lighten the dark night of despair and sin. A Cross on which there is no Figure may be a truer reminder of what Christ did than a Crucifix that tells always of pain and death.

While He is still on the Cross Christ says, "It is finished." What is finished? What does it mean actually to us that He said, "It is finished"? I have never thought that our Lord was referring to His own suffering. I have always thought the "It" referred to something that was holding me. I could imagine a father saying the same to his son on the morning that, after a long term in prison, he was allowed once more to join himself to his fellow men. The boy is free now—free, if he so cares, to make good and to live once more in the company of free men. He could fall back into the old grooves, or in the new life he could be born again. The way is not clear, but it is open.

I have read many books on the Atonement, and yet I cannot tell you much about it. I only know as the surest thing in the world that because Christ suffered I can love God, and because He came down to my level I have the power to rise toward His. If you love Jesus you are glad that He chose the Cross. It is more like Him than anything else He ever did. You will acknowledge, too, that in your case it has been effective, though you will stumble when you try to explain the how and why. The whole question that the Cross asks and answers is simply this: Will a man take Jesus at His word and commit himself to God? Will he hazard that the values of God are what Jesus said they were? These values are seen on the Cross.

Our Master taught that he who would be in the Kingdom of God must be the servant of all, and that although goodness, beauty, truth and humility can be crucified, they must inevitably rise again. It is a matter for us of experiment rather than argument. The man who will venture not half-way but the whole in daring to accept the new values of God will know that he was justified in his adventure.

Jesus said all sorts of lovely things would happen to those who would end the old and begin the new. The son would be home again and the father would cry, "He was lost and is found. Let us be merry." The son is now more God's than ever, just as a sheep that had been lost would be of greater value than one that had never strayed from home.

I have been over the world and have spent much time in watching people pursue happiness which all the while was by their side, or rather in their hearts for the bringing out. I have never met any as happy as those who have set out to prove that when God promised power to all who would be born again into the spirit of service, He said what He was perfectly able to carry out and by some grace indefinable that flows like a blessing from Calvary.

All this I hear as Jesus says from the Cross, "It is finished." Those words seem to imply, "And now it is up to you to begin. Those chains that hold you, test them, they cannot hold you any longer. That restless soul of yours that is always wanting you know not what —it was made for me. My peace I give unto you—if only you will take it." "It is finished" is the worker's cry of achievement which will be mocked at always by those who are unwilling to test its truth. Our moral difficulties come long before our intellectual ones. They are much the harder of the two. It is harder to forget self than to believe in miracles or repeat a Creed. Just before the darkness of death settles down, Christ tells us that He has set at liberty those that are bound and opened the road to the adventurous and unafraid.

There is no prospect ahead of us more glorious than the sense of comradeship with a great leader in a great crusade for the welfare of mankind. That is Christ's offer, and because He has made it, here one and here another join themselves to His company and find the road hard indeed, but infinitely worth while.

In *The Pilgrim's Progress* the story of the Atonement is well translated: "By what they say I perceive that he had been a great Warrior and had fought with and slain him that had the power of death, but not without great danger to himself, which made me love him the more."

27. THE NEED FOR IDEALISM[1]

In the nineteenth century, so I have read, the merchants of Liverpool gave a gold casket to the Prince Regent, for his endeavors to maintain against Wilberforce and Clarkson what the economists and merchants called the essential foundation of England's commercial prosperity, the slave trade. In those days, the experts and the economists were on one side, and the idealists and the agitators on the other. Lord Morley, commenting on this fact, writes: "Most of what is decently good in our curious world has been done by those two much abused sets of folk."

Experts and idealists are still often opposed, and it is profoundly important that those who profess Christianity should be numbered in the ranks of the latter, and that they should not mind being laughed at for refusing at times to accept the current opinions of the expert.

A great obstacle to Christian progress today is that attitude of humorous derision with which men are wont to kill idealism. Nearly every great movement has had to fight for its life against ridicule. After the Crimean War an attempt was made to start a League of Nations. It was laughed out of court. Whatever may be thought about Prohibition and Temperance, it will be admitted that one effective way in which people oppose it is by ridicule, for instance, by laughing at Mr. Pussyfoot Johnson. In this way English people have often killed the thing of which they are rather afraid.

It must be easy for a man to become cynical who does not believe in spiritual values, but it ought not to be possible for Christians. "You cannot change human nature" is not only the greatest lie, but the most damaging assertion. Under the protection of that falsehood a thousand men daily give way to lust, and with that as an excuse all sorts of

[1] From *St. Martin's Review* (London), June, 1922.

incredible follies and evils that are perfectly preventable are tolerated. Such phrases as "Men will be men" make it possible for certain evils to continue.

It must be realized that a faith in Jesus Christ carries with it a belief in the inherent goodness of all men and women, and an infinite belief in the possibility of a nobler and a better world. Our Lord, all through His life, kept on insisting on His Father's desire, not merely to patch up a breaking world, but to renovate, reform, and redeem it.

It is hard to hold on to ideals. Time after time faith seems to be shattered by the selfishness of public men, and the disappointing failures of personal and trusted friends. Unless a man is happy enough to have an ideal home for himself, how can he believe in the old-fashioned happiness of home life when the papers daily record the divorce of those who once were lovers? How can he believe in the integrity of politicians, when personal quarrels are given greater prominence than principles? How can he believe at all in these days in progress, when everywhere there seems a tendency, in Church and State alike, to revert to conditions that, during the war, men promised and swore to change, because it was known then that they were wrong. What has happened to the universally applauded suggestions for the reunion of Christendom? What has happened to those new ideals for co-operation in industry, to which so much lip service was given? The truth is that it is not realized that these things are possible, and things do not happen unless people know that they can, and mean that they shall.

We are all in it; we have fallen under the spell of a daily press that is almost entirely materialistic in its outlook, and a modern literature that has very little use for moral values, and very little faith or belief in any kind of idealism. Divorce, cup ties, Bottomley, these are the things that excite us. Unlike the old-fashioned novels, the modern novel, that deals almost exclusively with sex problems, does not send us back refreshed and encouraged for the battle of daily life. There seems no sort of criterion of what is good and what is bad. One does not know who selects the kind of things that are now forced upon our notice. It seems little short of arrant humbug that bookstalls that have decided to protect our minds by refusing to give publicity to *The Daily Herald*, should not hesitate to display *The Tatler, The Sketch,* and *The Bystander,* the three papers, I believe, that, by the illustration they give of ostentation, breed at least as much bad spirit as almost any other literature. While they prevent their stalls from offering us the point of view of Labor—roughly put often as it is—they do not hesitate to poison countless minds by the offer of a book by an ex-Prime Minister's daughter which, I think, without exception, is the most unwholesome piece of modern literature it has ever been my misfortune to come across.

This kind of thing does make it extremely difficult for men to hold on to their ideals. It does affect public opinion. We are caught in the spell of it, old and young alike. It seems as though there is hardly any place for idealism and nobility today. Surely it is foolish to believe in goodness at all. Man is fundamentally selfish. "You cannot change human nature." Thus it was and thus it will be. Class hatred, the sin of separation, slums, war, pestilences, selfishness and lust must continue.

We must resist in God's name the temptation that is always attacking us, to lose our faith in ideals. We must be ready to bank on idealism, to cry for the moon, to insist on obtaining the moon; to believe in noble things; to believe in people; to believe that every person's motive is as honest as that which we attribute to ourselves. Wherever we meet a person young or old, who is holding on to what is noble and pure and of good report, we must never, never by any word whatsoever, tend to undermine that faith; never hurt, or cut by cruel cynicism or bitter humor; never, never, damp any enthusiasm for what is noble and great by that dreadful phrase: "When I was your age I believed in that too." All that is best in this curious old world of ours has been achieved by agitators and idealists, in the face, nearly always, of experts, but in the end it will always be the idealists that will win. As one thinks of the crucified Lord on the Cross, one knows it. Those who believe that human nature and human conditions can be changed are the only people who are ever likely to change them. Whenever our faith in idealism is gone, we have ceased to believe in goodness, whatever creed we profess, we have ceased to believe in the Christian God.

Our business is, so far as we can, to leaven public opinion with Christian optimism.

Public opinion is, after all, the power that gets things done, for good or evil, and in public opinion the individual is really the important factor. For all practical purposes, we are public opinion, and it is our primary duty to create a public opinion that believes and follows after Christian idealism.

In our march through life we shall generally find what we are looking for. If we are looking for trouble we shall nearly always find it. If we are looking at our neighbor with a view to seeing what is wrong in him, we shall find plenty. If all men are looking with suspicion at their neighbors they will never see the good in them. They will never understand their position. They will never know or love them.

If there is that in us which bristles up the moment we approach those with whom we do not agree they will have no contribution to give to us, and there is no soul in the world whose offering we do not need. The fault of those who are intent on good works, is that we always wait in our study to do good to someone who comes to us. The attitude which we should attempt to reach is that when someone comes to us, he or she is going first of all to teach us. You hear people say, "I have got to go to the hospital; so and so wants to see me," with no sort of conception of what that life may have to teach: or "I have to go to see a fallen woman," with no conception of the lesson that child of God may have to give. The world would be so different if we did not always think we were called to teach everybody else; if we realized that we never met a soul, rich or poor, high or low, degraded or noble, who had not some lesson to teach us, and that a lesson which we badly needed.

How bitter must be the heart of every idealist who finds his dream of Utopia laughed at, and how hard it must be to hold on to that dream, and to work and toil for it in the face of ridicule. We realize the platitude that it is only Christian principles that can achieve industrial or international peace, but do we realize that there are still countless professing Christians who are smiling cynically at the mention of the League of Nations, and suggesting that human nature, being what it is, there must always be antagonism between classes and peoples and races? That is a negation of our Christian optimism, a negation of our God.

If religion in these days has nothing to offer except a series of Prayer Book Services for those who are that way inclined, if it has no high belief and passion in idealism, if it does not believe that the so-called impossible can be attained by those whose hearts are set on God, if it never hears its Lord Jesus Christ from the Cross and from the empty tomb claiming the whole world as His own, if it does not shout with those who tell out their dream of a time when the sword shall be turned into the ploughshare, and men and women shall dwell together in peace and unity—then all these Sunday observances of ours are a mockery, and the body of Christ is dead, and the spirit of Christ must move through some other channel.

We must not, then, mind aiming at the stars. We may not hit them. We probably shall not. But at least we shall pierce the cloud that envelops them and hides their light. We must believe in ideals: believe in men and women. Remember that to our Lord they were the beings most like God. The background of their lives is always white; never black. Because He believed in them He cried: "The Kingdom of God is at hand." On the day when we recapture our belief in idealism, the Kingdom of God will be at hand. It may not have arrived, but at least it will be assured. As far as in us lies we must always "set up a mark of everlasting light above the howling senses' ebb and flow." That poem of Matthew Arnold's is well worth remembering.

28. THE OPEN SECRET OF CHRISTMAS[1]

To many observers Christmas must seem like a fit of madness which comes over us for a brief season when the days are short and the nights long and cold. If self-interest is the law of human life, and peace on the earth is a dream, and not even a lovely dream, then this outburst of good will must be entirely foolish and insane. It is a holiday from business; an escape from school! Why is man unable to renounce these wild joys and dreams? What is it that prompts him to set out once more with wise men and shepherds for Bethlehem? Why does man go mad once a year?

There is another possibility. What if man comes to his senses at Christmas? What if he is mad when he scorns love and fights for his own selfish interests? What if he is sinning against the very nature of things, when he hates and fights, and will not be at peace with his fellows? At any rate this is a possible explanation. The real life of mankind may be that which he sees and adores at Christmastide; and the other life may be wild, mad, and suicidal. It may be that the dreamer is the one who is awake to realities, and the plain matter-of-fact man is asleep. The holiday may be the real working time; and the school from which we escape an Asylum!

The secret of Christmas need not be dismissed on the ground that it is simple. All the great discoveries by which the human mind has advanced into the mysteries of the world are simple, though they open out endless new ways into the unknown. The last secret of the universe may be so simple that we may easily miss it. Our Lord declared that these things are hidden from the wise and prudent and revealed unto babes; the wise and prudent may come into the inheritance, but only as they have the heart of the child. It is an open secret which is

---
[1] From *St. Martin's Review* (London), December, 1924.

ours at Christmastide; the wise may ponder upon all that is implied in it; they may think out its expressions, but the secret itself is not reserved for them; it is the Word which comes to all men, who are humble enough to receive it.

> Go humbly; humble are the skies
> And low and large and fierce the Star;
> So very near the Manger lies
> That we may travel far.[2]

But do we need any secret at all? Is Western civilization built upon certain solid unsentimental, hard principles, which act well? What other secret can there be than that men should consider only their own self-interests, and in defence of them should wield their glittering swords? The answer to such claims can be put in one word "Europe!" An interpretation of human life can scarcely be called satisfying, which has brought Europe to its present estate.

Or if we care to look into the condition of Great Britain, we cannot boast that we have found the secret of human society in our industrial and social order. Whatever can be claimed by those who reject the Christian principle, they cannot delude us into thinking that the counterprinciples work out in practice. "Love, generosity, humility," they tell us, "are very well in theory, but as practical men we cannot accept them."

Hatred, selfishness, pride—do these really work well in human affairs? They bring happiness neither to those who win in the conflict nor to those who lose. We can approach Christmas as seekers with a problem weighing upon us which at least is not solved. If there is a secret, we shall not refuse to consider it on the ground that we know all that is necessary already. Other ways have proved illusory. Other lords have failed us. The common-sense of materialism has proved folly. Its promises have been broken. The wisdom of this world has turned out to be madness. Perhaps the "foolishness of God" may be the one thing needful.

We are not going mad at Christmastide. We are enjoying a lapse into sanity. We are not letting ancient racial emotions take us from the right path of human progress; we are entering for a brief time into the glories of the age to come, when man will come to himself. Christmastide is a pledge of the great age to come.

[2] Mr. G. K. Chesterton.

The Eternal Love came down at Christmas. The Word of Love came to us in the only way in which it could come. The Word became flesh and dwelt among us. The God Who made the stars cares for man, seeks him, shares his life, redeems him through the Son of His love. That He should come in this way is wonderful; but if He is love it is simple to understand; it may be for some too good to be true, but it cannot be too difficult to understand. If there is a Love at the heart of all things, it is by this way and this way only He must come. Love cannot be revealed otherwise in all its yearning, and in all its passion.

But open as this secret now is to the seekers who gather by the Manger, it will never be perfectly manifest, till men believe that Love like that is the very *groundwork of human life*, and the very life principle of human society, and till they act as though this Love were the common sense which alone can save mankind.

At any rate there is an opening for this new secret. Other hopes have failed mankind. We cannot afford to continue living on the practical maxims of the world. We cannot afford to hate one another. We need some other principle by means of which we can at least make more hopeful experiments. The idealists may prove to be wrong, but the others *are* wrong. Certain "hard-headed" men declare that the teaching of Jesus is not fitted for a world like this. What is perfectly certain is that the methods of the hard-headed are not fitted for a world like this. They at least have broken down. Why not go mad with Christ for a change? Once more; we do not approach the wonder of Christmas as those who can afford to scorn that strange revelation of Love Incarnate. It may prove to be illusory, we shall know better when we have tried it. The Lord Christ *may* prove a vain hope, but one thing is clear, all the others who have defied Him, and ignored Him have already been proved to be false prophets.

He is the last resort, is He? Others might resent that, but He will not. Man will only have Him when he has no other to try! It is enough for Him that soon or late man shall know His need and accept Him. In the words of Mr. Chesterton

> When we could not fly from Thee anywhere
> We fled to Thee.

It comes to this; for Christmastide we shall become little children again; we shall cast out bitterness, we shall establish in our heart true relations with all men, even Germans and Russians; at least there will be no bitterness proceeding from us to them. We shall cease to talk of class wars, or to think in terms of classes. We shall see a glory around all little children. We shall take a holiday from selfishness. We shall love others as Our Lord has loved us. A brief mad episode!

But is this Lord of Love with His secret only to tarry with us for a few days? Shall we then bid Him good-by at the door as though He had been a guest welcomed in His coming, but only for an appointed time?

Love is of God; and everyone that loveth is born of God. Love is the way for man; and everyone that loveth has the secret of this earthly life both for himself and for all human society. At Christmas, dimly or clearly, all men see this. It is a fine opportunity for those who care for the Christian Gospel. They dwell in the midst of men who are in the grasp of a noble emotion. They share an undying memory; they are dreaming again the lost dreams of childhood; they see the world through the eyes of those upon whom Jesus saw resting the radiance of the heavenly country. If only they could be encouraged to keep mad! If only they would make this holiday from the tyranny of the world a continuous thing! If only they would refuse to go back to the establishment of the world! For a short time we understand the folly of the world which in its wisdom knows not God. It only remains for us, denying all other gods, to carry the secret of the Love which came down at Christmas into all the doings of all the year. This is reality; this is eternal life.

29. WE MUST NOT FORGET[1]

Some time ago a youngster who lived in a mean street was having an unusually rough time. He was hero, or fool enough (which you will) to hang on to his ideals, even to his religion.

They didn't at all approve of that in the factory where he worked, and he got his daily dose of ridicule and abuse.

One day one of the crowd said to him: "You blankety fool, can't you see that if there is a God who cares tuppence for the likes of you He'd tell someone to come along and give you what you need—decent food, a bed to yourself, and at least the chance of making good."

To this the youngster replied: "I reckon He does tell someone, only someone always forgets."

None too bad an answer. I suppose the reason so many perfectly preventable evils persist at all ends of the town is because such a number of us "always forget."

It was once said about the English by a foreigner, that their main vice consisted not in doing evil but in permitting it. Certainly we find certain social evils too unpleasant to talk about, but not too unpleasant to forget.

It seems that even our public bodies and corporations (not excluding churches), have a way of forgetting those whom they were called into being to remember—and save.

A hardening, inhuman process sets in, and after that the institution is liable to remember no one and nothing, except that its own life and prestige must be preserved at all costs.

Beverley Nichols recently suggested that "every discussion of poverty should *begin* with the realization of empty stomachs and squalid rooms, and should *end* with statistics," and that "all parliamentary

[1] From *Some of My Religion*, Harper & Brothers (New York, 1936).

debates on unemployment relief should be carried on in the sombre and fetid atmosphere of a Glasgow slum."

There could be no forgetting in such surroundings. We cannot all take a hand in humanizing and debunking institutions, but most of us could pull considerable weight if we would remember those whose welfare, struggle or sorrow we ought never to have forgotten.

It is just decent human understanding, not charity, that our neighbor —like ourself—needs.

The man who said indignantly: "Am I my brother's keeper?" was a bad lot. It is a poor, ungrateful, unsocial business to be numbered among those who "always forget."

As to our institutions, even they would work well enough and remember their purpose afresh if a sufficient number of citizens cared to see that they should.

30. THE MINISTRY OF ART[1]

A great writer, who is also a considerable musician, told me recently that, if he were able, he would give up writing prose and attempt instead to express himself through the medium of some other art; music for preference.

"For," said he, "a musician, in a bar or two, may say what it will take an author a thousand words to say less satisfactorily."

The critic who declared that an Englishman would rather listen to Offenbach than Bach often may be allowed his little joke, and yet most of us would confess that there are occasions when good music can tell us worth-while things with a directness denied to any sequence of words.

Browning said that a musician could say more than anyone else and Bach wrote a prayer in the margin of one of his fugues and then set it to music in an effort to explain it.

This is profoundly true about religion, as any man knows who prefers—and who does not?—the sound of a carol on Christmas Day to any treatise on the Incarnation by the vicar.

Nowhere is the sheer inadequacy of words more evident than in the presentation of Christianity.

Every Church is better than its official literature, simply because there is no such thing as a heavenly language.

Those who have seen what the saints call the beatific vision—explorers as great and greater than those who discover fresh territory—cannot find words in which to express what they have seen.

The technical language and jargon which every great cause begets becomes increasingly wearisome and irritating to the plain man: he does not know for the life of him what it is all about.

[1] From *Some of My Religion*, Harper & Brothers (New York, 1936).

I fear the vocabulary of the conventionally religious is no exception.

Unfortunately there is scarcely a phrase current among those who support Churches that has not either been distorted by controversy, or embedded in the smoke and gas which the contending schools of thought have given off; so that many deeply religious people, and many whom the Germans call "Christians in unconsciousness," hesitate to use the approved vocabulary of religion lest they should be misunderstood and add to the existing confusion.

It's a bad and sad business: no wonder that religious writers sometimes feel that the wealth, the simplicity, and the mysticism of Christianity might be commended more readily by art than by words.

Perhaps the satisfactory compromise would arrive if no one who was not half a poet and half a musician were permitted to deal in theology.

The Founder of Christianity was a divine artist. (Who else in that day could have made that exquisite comparison between Solomon in all his glory and the flowers of the field?)

It is a soul and not a system that we find in the words of Jesus Christ.

We shall never understand His teaching unless and until we divorce it from that sometimes terrible atmosphere of repression and severity in which mankind is accustomed to hear it proclaimed.

Our Lord was and is the Eternal Voice calling to all men everywhere, not to do awkward unnatural things—like performing animals at their tricks—so that later they may be rewarded, but to be what all men in their best moments really desire to be, sons and daughters of a God as lovable as was the father in the story of the Prodigal Son— our Father which art in Heaven.

Whatever the highbrows may say, the Christianity of Jesus Christ is more akin to a light in a cottage window on a dark night than any light that may be shed from some professorial study or lecture room.

We must serve God with head as well as heart, but it was not of theological light that Jesus Christ was speaking when He said: "Let your light so shine before men."

Yet even as I write these simple words I realize how easily they may be misunderstood and sentimentalized.

Perhaps it is true that the height, the breadth and the depth of the love of God in Christ Jesus awaits our understanding until its dull prose becomes more like great music.

31. MUST THE CHURCH COMPROMISE?[1]

The question of whether it is desirable that churches should be better attended on Sundays depends, of course, on the quality of the religion they present.

This problem was sympathetically discussed, not so very long ago, in the leading column of a daily newspaper, and the article concluded with the suggestion that if the churches are to be attractive, and attendance at them increased, there must be "a new tremendous effort to prove that they stand for what they profess—for peace and good will, for loving kindness and *for no compromise* (my italics) with the countering forces of war, brutality, and oppression."

Few who know their way about organized religion will dispute the need for this "new tremendous effort," but they may question if the result would fill the churches.

I am inclined to think that if organized Christianity went "all out" for the religion of Jesus Christ the churches would be a great deal emptier than they are now.

What I have to say is not intended as a censure on my neighbor, for we are all involved in this grave problem, and which of us today is willing to cast a stone at our fellows?

I yield to none in my belief in the goodness of ordinary people, but I fancy most of us still fail to realize that the Christian religion is a terrific, lovely, explosive, world-shattering force, and not an anodyne against life's little or large disturbances.

The "Magnificat" is as much more revolutionary as it is more beautiful than "The Red Flag," and it is only because we sing it without thought that we fail to realize the fact.

When Christianity was perfectly presented "many went back and

---

[1] From *Some of My Religion*, Harper & Brothers (New York, 1936).

walked no more with Him"; and if today the loving, charitable flaming awe-ful Word of God were cried aloud in the churches, there would be no shambles at their doors on the part of those who sought admission.

My desire is not to dogmatize, but (if I may) to induce people to think about religion.

It will be a painful process for all of us, for as a wise man once said: "When we learn something new it always seems at first as if we had lost something old."

In the matter of Christianity I suggest that it is high time that we all—not excluding parsons—should determine whether we desire and would support a Christian Church that would risk and give its life, as its Lord did; rather than compromise with the will of God, or whether we should prefer some mild and manageable version of religion that would be willing to make us comfortable and call our pagan emotions by gentle names: our hatred of others, passion for righteousness; our denominational preferences, eternal truth; our lust for revenge, zeal for justice; our pride, proper self-respect; our cowardice and lack of passion, statesmanlike caution and wisdom; our abominable lethargy in the face of perfectly preventable evils, the recognition that only fools step in where angels fear to tread; and, lastly, our sin, the unavoidable accident of daily living.

If in our immediate neighborhood we had opportunity to support one of these two so-called presentations of Christianity, which (if either) should we choose?

I do not think it would be an exaggeration to suggest that the future of civilization depends on man's answer to this mighty problem.

32. SIMPLIFY CHRISTIANITY![1]

The English are essentially reverent-minded and do not expect religion to be anything but a serious affair.

They have no preference for stunting Churches or parsons "playing to the gallery."

Even if they had their preference should not be encouraged.

Better shut the churches and stone the prophets than suffer them to compete for popularity with the local cinema or other places of entertainment.

No great cause can hope for long to hold the allegiance of the virile that in a desire, however amiable, to win converts makes light of its essential notes of sternness and urgency.

This is supremely true about Christianity, and fortunately the Englishman is perfectly aware of it. Unless I am gravely mistaken, when he attends church he does not really require what is merely bright and breezy, but something strong and manifestly sincere; in form, dignified; in content, charitable; in expression, level with his understanding; in length, merciful.

He will not even object to what is called mysticism, provided he be convinced that something wholly worth while is going forward.

And yet before the ink dries on that last sentence, let me rush on to plead, with all the force of which I am capable, for the drastic and immediate simplification of official Christianity.

It is monstrous that we should have suffered it to become as complicated as it now is.

It is an adventure in living, and not an intellectual orthodoxy to which the Churches should summon mankind.

No one who has lived with his fellows in recent years can possibly suggest that they have turned their backs on God and goodness; if

---
[1] From *Some of My Religion*, Harper & Brothers (New York, 1936).

they are ceasing to attend churches, and they certainly are, may it not be because of what is best, not because of what is worst, in them?

Men and women are finding it increasingly hard to believe that the Pearl of infinite price can be hidden within that dry, dull and dusty field of loveless inhuman orthodoxy in which they are so often bidden to seek it.

Today the religion of the Churches has become so highly complicated, so largely academic, so much at the mercy of its experts with their technical terms, that plain folk just don't know what to make of it, what it is all about.

As well expect a newborn baby to thrive on a lump of ice as a stranger to feel at home and find his Lord in the atmosphere of some churches and chapels.

Here, scores of religious people will wish to say to me with indignation: "Even if this be true—and we deny it—why write about it—why bring your soiled linen for the public to gaze upon?"

To this I am obliged to answer that I am now, alas, convinced that there are certain scandals so ominous, and to which we have become so accustomed, that they will never be attended to until they are dragged into the market place for inspection.

If there be any greater scandal in these grave days than that of freezing over a way by which the Saviour and Lover of Men could come again, compellingly to call His own to save their world and follow Him in incorruptness, I know it not.

The most enheartening sound that could be heard in the land today would be that of the coming together of all the religious; leaders, parsons, and people, that they might consider an agenda on which one item only appeared:—

"To make the religion of Jesus Christ and its official presentation—with the Cross at its center—simpler, larger, more charitable, more human, so that all men of good will everywhere might hear in their own tongue the wonderful works of God."

I would turn the key on the religions and keep them at it until they had solved this problem, which is perfectly soluble, save for the hardness of our hearts.

Would not this simplification of Christianity be according to the mind of Christ, Who, in His earthly pilgrimage, strove passionately and persistently to deliver the hungry crowd from the indigestible subtleties of many of their professional teachers?

33. HUMAN NATURE CAN CHANGE[1]

Many excellent people suffer themselves to be overawed by sayings, called axioms, saws, even truisms, which are just sufficiently true to be dangerously deceptive.

We allow those sayings to close and clinch argument—like old Euclid's Q.E.D.

My concern now is with that hoary old saw about the unchangeableness of human nature. In its smug and accepted form—"You cannot change human nature"—it is not only untrue, but arrant nonsense besides.

We use it as a cloak for our lusts, for sins of commission, and equally for the blistering sins of omission which permit perfectly remediable evils to flourish.

"You cannot change human nature," and therefore wars, unemployment, slums, graft, exploitation and every other iniquity must continue until the crack of doom.

If men, women and children are damned of body and soul by the conditions under which they live and work, it is highly regrettable—a great pity—"but," so the pompous gas-bag continues, "I'm a realist, I am, not like those blankety dreamers; I take *facts* into consideration, I do, and I tell you that human nature never alters, never changes. So that's that"—Q.E.D.

Are we to sit quiet under this paralyzing stuff about the unchangeableness of human nature? God forbid.

But what is the answer?

Will those who know forgive me suggesting a line to any who may be puzzled? If my prescription be condensed, as the space at my dis-

---
[1] From *Some of My Religion*, Harper & Brothers (New York, 1936).

posal entails, it can yet be made up powerfully for those who will receive it into their systems.

May I suggest to any who are worried by the old saying about human nature that:

(1) When you hear men say: "You cannot change human nature," you should ask politely but firmly what the dickens is actually meant by that phrase? I do not fancy they will have any rejoinder to make except that human conduct and behavior never change, which, of course, is frankly a lie.

(2) Remind them of such old-fashioned trifles as cannibalism, slavery, torture, duelling. What has happened to them and why?

(3) You may now desire to touch upon experience in your lifetime, of the growth of sobriety, of the more understanding attitude toward children, of the more humane treatment of criminals, and of the kindlier behavior toward animals. However these results have been obtained, it cannot be denied by anyone outside Bedlam that they have happened because what is called human nature has changed. We are not what we were.

(4) How about suggesting next that human conduct is so plastic that it can be, and is, molded almost out of recognition by individuals as well as by institutions, by prophets, parsons, physicians, professors, philanthropists, politicians, and even by policemen?

(5) Here let me slip in a caution. You will be careful to admit frankly and fearlessly that "human nature" may alter for the worse, as well as for the better, while remembering that on this occasion you are not dealing with the question of its direction, but whether or not it can change and be directed.

(6) Lastly: You will not make light of what it costs a man or a nation to alter habits, or fail to acknowledge that when you and I have driven out the tiger and the ape from within us that intractable animal the donkey—as was once suggested—may still survive.

It will generally be found that all who wish to lend a hand are singularly like-minded whatever creed they profess. If Christians once got going and busy they could soon tear out by the roots those crimes that now disgrace our civilization.

It is unthinkable that they should be overawed any longer by that old bogey about human nature being unchangeable. One breath of the spirit of our Lord, and even of common sense, would blast it sky-high.

34. WHAT WOULD LONDON DO TO CHRIST?[1]

It is hard to prophesy what our Lord would say to London were He to come in the flesh, but fairly easy to guess what London would say to Him.

God alone knows what Christ would make of us, but we know pretty accurately what we should make of Him.

Undoubtedly His arrival would throw us into much the same confusion as occurred precisely at eleven o'clock on November 11, 1918.

We should cast our work and play to the winds, leave home or office to wander among our fellows, inquiring of every passer-by what was the meaning of this portentous advent that had dawned in our winter sky.

What did it forebode? How eagerly we should await the evening papers to explain or explain Him away; doubtless the bewildered leader-writers would already be hard at work buzzing inquiries along the lines that connect Fleet Street with Lambeth.

For ourselves, we should be strangely elated and strangely confused. It would be most disintegrating, for although for years we have been asking for a man, the arrival of the One who, by instinct rather than by orthodoxy, we have long called The Man is surely a little sudden and premature.

And yet without doubt He comes in the fullness of time, for the world is in dire need of repair; the voices of its chosen counselors have lost their ring of confidence.

But, still, earthquakes are not in our line. Here is the setting in which the Christ is to take the center of the stage.

And at first all will go well. There will be an immediate success,

---
[1] From *Some of My Religion*, Harper & Brothers (New York, 1936).

WHAT WOULD LONDON DO TO CHRIST?

and if the Prophet wear an Eastern garment we shall be the more diverted, for we are fond of novelties in our religion.

But a check soon happens, for nothing very startling and miraculous takes place, and the remnant that remains is sifted and thinned still further at the first appeal for individual righteousness.

I think that we should soon be saying that our Lord is disappointing and curiously ineffective.

As a social reformer, He lacks a programme; as an orator, He is unconvincing: a good man, no doubt, but unpractical and unwise.

Obviously He loves deeply, almost desperately, but His speech is careless and too spontaneous, it lends itself to misunderstanding.

He talks nothing but the dialect of the human heart, very persuasively, but it is rather embarrassing, and too painfully direct. Altogether an interesting and considerable personage, but—forgive us hazarding the suggestion—is He not just a little extravagant and emotional?

And one cannot run this modern world on extravagance and emotion.

Why, once He blazed out at a number of quite excellent people who were merely tightening up their creed in the interest of religion itself, and twice He was seen to cry in public, once in Park Lane, and again in Poplar.

Clearly, too, He is no match for the learned. He will not counter their arguments with arguments of His own.

He says that it is useless to argue with those who will not unlearn, and He merely tells them to forget their dull theories and to think instead of men, women and children.

After which He passes on to a company of people who are not nearly so worth while, indeed rather a second-rate lot.

And He makes the mistake of allowing passion to creep into His message. He says that only through passion can man attain to wisdom and that God is as passionate as the Father in the story of the Prodigal Son.

He says that the cold wisdom of this world is lunacy, and that sanity comes as surely from warmth as insanity from coldness.

He bids men be passionate, and, of course, that is a great mistake and a little dangerous.

A man whose message is colored by his emotions is not a safe guide. And then there is one other factor, and this, I fear, is determining.

It is found that our Lord is not really English: He is not wholly devoted to our British interests.

Not being "sound" here is fatal. For some little time He has been suspect and this is just too much.

London is genuinely sorry to lose so gracious and well-meaning a figure, but it would be best for Him to leave.

Anyhow, with much courtesy we should ask our Lord to leave our coasts, for a time at any rate.

And meanwhile, to placate His strange followers, we might appoint a committee of erudite ecclesiastics, with a Privy Councillor or two and, of course, one woman and one representative of Labor to assist, to investigate with a view to obtaining from His teaching some practical scheme which would be generally acceptable for national improvement and international security.

I am not being censorious—God knows I have no right to be. But this is what I really believe London would do to our Lord.

35. THE LONELY[1]

Not so very long ago I came on this, from the writings of Rupert Brooke:

"I haven't told you much about my voyage, have I? There's not much to tell. I felt a trifle lonely before I left Liverpool; everybody seemed to have people to see them off. So I went back on shore and found a dirty little boy, who was unoccupied and said his name was William.

"'Will you wave to me if I give you sixpence, William?' I said. 'Why, yes,' said William.

"So I gave him sixpence and went on board. When the time came he leaned over the railing on the landing stage and waved.

"Now and then he shouted indistinct messages in a shrill voice. And as we slid away the last object I saw was a small dot waving a white handkerchief, nearly white, faithfully.

"So I got my sixpenn'orth and my farewell—dear William!"

What a dreadful thing is loneliness, and how many of us need a William.[2]

Our teachers have told us time and again to cultivate the art of being happy alone, but there are occasions when it cannot be done, and when we suspect that even they—for all their brave words—are not able to practise what they preach.

The trouble is that there are so many forms of loneliness, and when we have beaten back one or two, on comes another ugly fellow and finds a lodgment where he has no right to be.

There are some people who say they are never lonely, but it will generally be found that these have a busy or happy background to

---
[1] From *Some of My Religion*, Harper & Brothers (New York, 1936).
[2] *Memoirs*, Sidgwick & Jackson (London).

their lives, in which case they have never really understood what aloneness means.

Those who are fortunate in this respect cannot realize what men and women suffer who really are alone.

In a sense, every thinking person must at times endure a feeling of isolation.

There is the inescapable loneliness of the great, or rather of the large mind.

A man like Napoleon must have been envied when he was in the full flood of his triumphs, but there can be no doubt that he knew, as few other men have known, what it was to be lonely. It is probably true that the dictators of the present day like Mussolini, Stalin, and Hitler must sometimes be intolerably aware that they are alone.

There are words that Bernard Shaw has put into the mouth of Joan of Arc which poignantly reveal the loneliness of a great soul.

Facing her accusers she cries: "I am alone on earth: I have always been alone. . . . My father told my brother to drown me if I would not stay to mind his sheep while France was bleeding to death: France might perish if only our lambs were safe. . . .

"Do not think you can frighten me by telling me that I am alone. France is alone; and God is alone; and, what is my loneliness before the loneliness of my country and my God?

"I see now that the loneliness of God is His strength: what would He be if He listened to your jealous little counsels?

"Well, my loneliness shall be my strength too: it is better to be alone with God: His friendship will not fail me, nor His counsel, nor His love."[3]

What about the unspeakable loneliness of Christ?

"What, could ye not watch with Me one hour?" We lesser folk can know but little of the loneliness of the great.

Ours is of a different kind, but it hurts like fury for all that.

Many of my readers will know what it means to live in lodgings, in not too easy circumstances, and to return there in the evening with no welcome awaiting, no one to talk to, no money for the pictures, no consolation at home except the gas ring.

It must be nearly as bad to be alone in a luxury flat.

And how lonely a great city can be—the gossip of a village is better

---

[3] *St. Joan,* Constable (London).

THE LONELY

than the utter loneliness of a town that knows and cares nothing about our comings and goings.

And there is a still worse form of loneliness—and I have been meeting it lately at night in the crypt of a certain church that is always open—it is the loneliness of feeling that no one in the wide world wants you, even as a "hand" for work, let alone as a heart to love.

That is the outside misery of existence which many suffer today. It's as near hell as anything in this world can be.

A few nights ago I was talking to yet another stranger, who told me that for months he had wandered around London looking for work.

And what had seared his very soul was not so much that he had not found work, but that nowhere had he found a word of kindness.

Was he exaggerating? Let us hope so, but years ago, when I lived in East London, I often accompanied men early in the morning on their dreary tramp in search of employment, and often I was shocked and surprised beyond words at the thoughtless way in which their applications would be turned down with one abrupt sentence.

An equally short one with a "Sorry, old man, and good luck," would have made all the difference in the world—the difference between the applicant going away disappointed, or going away feeling utterly alone and unwanted—suicidal.

There is not a great deal we can do to cure our neighbor's loneliness, we are hard pressed enough at times to help our own.

But at least we could be on the lookout, where we live, to see if there is anyone near by whom we could help without patronage.

And, at least, if any should approach us seeking such service as might dispel their sense of isolation we could send them away—if send them away we must—with the belief that, at any rate, one person seemed to understand and to regret being unable to help.

This is one of the elementary things that every professing Christian should take in his stride.

36. A WORD TO THE CRITICS[1]

It is high time someone said something about the critics of organized Christianity. They often spoil their case by the extravagance of their language and the generally uninformed and mutually destructive nature of their complaints. Perhaps it is natural that the Churches should have their full share of abuse, only it need not be overdone, and it should not be carried to the point of abusing them for things which they are not doing or, except in rare instances, saying. As a matter of fact the Christian Churches are thoroughly aware of their shortcomings and were so a considerable time ago. I believe they are more genuinely anxious to return to the ideals which they have never wholly forsworn than any other groups in public life which exist for the welfare of mankind. There would be more ground for hope if others were equally well aware of their shortcomings. Whatever may be said about the National Mission of Repentance and Hope, which for instance was carried through by the Church of England in the early days of war, it was at least a mission of repentance—that is of the recognition of a measure of failure.

The wildest flight of imagination cannot picture politicians and other parties of public servants daring to confess that they had missed the mark. If repentance is the beginning of amendment the Churches are a long way ahead of the State.

There is, or ought to be, a limit to the use of destructive criticism, and there is a danger that criticism which is pointful and relevant may be set aside if the language that conveys it is too extravagant. Of uninformed criticism there is no end. Anyone appears to be at liberty to write or speak about the "failure of Christianity." It is, apparently, the one branch of knowledge for which no training or

[1] From *St. Martin's Review* (London), February, 1923.

experience is essential. I have before me as I write criticisms which I have culled from time to time from the press during the last six years. A good many are evidently written by people who have in view a type of organized Christianity which, as a matter of plain fact, has never existed except in their own minds. Some are criticizing a type which did once exist but which no longer survives, and some a form of religion, which undoubtedly they have come across, but which would be repudiated by all except the obscurantists. But two things are especially noticeable. Most of the criticism is leveled at the heads of the clergy, and the clergy and the Church are looked upon as synonymous: for the rest the critics generally contradict each other. Here is a list of criticisms of a slightly more intelligent nature which will prove this contention.

The Church has failed—
1. Because it has ceased to be Catholic,
2. because it has ceased to be Protestant,
3. because during the war the clergy did not fight as combatants,
4. because some of them did,
5. because the clergy are too immersed in practical affairs,
6. because they are too immersed in what they call "matters that are spiritual,"
7. because there is too much dogma,
8. because there is not enough,
9. because the clergy are all of one class,
10. because the clergy are not of "the type they used to be."

It would be easy but unnecessary to prolong this list; on one point they agree, the "failure of the Church" is caused entirely by the clergy; apart from this it is impossible to effect any synthesis which can make all the criticisms agree.

It would be of some assistance and encouragement if the critics, who were nominally Christian and even members of a Christian Church, would include themselves in the charges that they bring against organized Christianity. It would be helpful if they would recognize that a great many criticisms must be wide of the mark if a great many others are true. Some of those (mostly the clergy of all denominations may it be said) who are endeavoring to make their Churches living centers of Truth and reality are not a little discouraged at the quantity of criticism of a not very helpful character that is showered upon them. It is easy to criticize—it is much more noble to assist. There are a great many critics who are like the people who grumble at Germany in wanting what they criticize not so much repentant and reformed as unrepentant and destroyed.

I grow more and more skeptical of that mass of men which is supposed to be standing in the anteroom of organized religion only waiting to pass into the fold until such time as the Churches are "brought into relation with modern needs and thought." For some it is more attractive to be in opposition than to accept the responsibility of service which is demanded of those within. I am naturally not here referring to those who are genuinely disturbed at their inability to accept the intellectual statements of Christianity.

Let those who think the Founder of Christianity is merely a dead figure of a bygone day say what they will. If they are honest in their opinions we have no ground to complain; but one may be permitted to grow increasingly wearied by the criticisms, uninformed and destructive as they are, of those who profess to desire that the Churches should save the soul of the World and yet will not do a hand's turn of work to that end.

Might I be allowed to suggest to some of the most confident that it would be well in the interest of intelligence to give up saying things about the Churches that thoughtful men have ceased to say even on platforms in Victoria Park, and to make their contribution to the reform of organized Christianity in some other way than by merely suggesting the destruction of everything that they have never taken the trouble to understand. There are many within the Churches passionately desirous of radical reform in their outlook and ceremonies; to those there is something bitterly disappointing in the type of criticism and, let it be added, in the character of the critics, who appear to know nothing except that they do not like what at the moment exists. The first step is to persuade them to cease using the terms Church and ministers of religion as synonymous and to study the subject they wish to criticize. Then we will gratefully listen to what they have to say.

37. RESPECT THE VIEWS OF THOSE WHO HATE PACIFISM[1]

Frankly, while I hold to the cause of Pacifism I am badly in need of wisdom on the whole subject. I believe—and shall continue to believe—that the ordinary honest man, who gave his life in the last War for what his conscience told him was right, was in all cases a martyr. In most cases he was an infinitely finer type than the majority, I only say the majority, of the Conscientious Objectors. It was my fault and the fault of other Christian teachers that we had not outlawed War in the years that preceded the time when it seemed inevitable even to high-minded people, i.e., August of 1914. Don't be cross with me for saying this, but while I am able to love Conscientious Objectors from afar, just as I am able to love Bulgars from afar, I cannot love them when I am in their presence either in Trafalgar Square or in Bulgaria. Is it possible to be a Pacifist by conviction and yet respect the views of some of those who hate pacifism? Perhaps it isn't, but that is where I stand. Certainly there is a very wicked doctrine called: "My Country—right or wrong," but there is also a very beastly doctrine called: "My Country—always wrong," which is all too prevalent today amongst the fanatics and freaks who rush into every progressive cause, getting badly in the way of its triumph. What *is* worrying me terribly is that, speaking generally, the youth of today, especially at the public schools, is still being taught patriotism in terms of war, when of course, except for the hardness of our hearts and the dullness of our understanding, it has nothing to do with war. I, too, believe that war can only be ended by some great Power laying down its life, as Christ did on the Cross,

---

[1] From *What Can We Believe?* edited by Laurence Housman, Jonathan Cape (London, 1939).

for the World's sake, and I, too, who yield to no one in love of my Country, would be proud if it went down for that great sake, and went down in history besides as the Great Empire that gave its very life so that the way of Christ, at least in one respect, might prevail.

38. HUMOR

SOMETHING TO TELL TO SAINT PETER

Once Dick's incurable human interest in other people put him in another plight from which honor allowed no retreat. He had to advance, even though the consequences might be disastrous. He was calling on an old lady who had asked him to tea. She was an ardent admirer of his, and so for a great treat she had winkles for tea. Dick examined the delicacy with doubt but an open mind. He picked a winkle up and examined it. "But how do you get them out?" he asked. His hostess with a shy and rapid gesture took a hairpin from her head and handed it across the table to her guest—"'Ere you are, duckie!" Dick took it and used it. He used to say, when he remembered it, that he would tell the tale to St. Peter, if there was any trouble at the gate. That would get him in, wouldn't it?[1]

Sidney Smith once said that he would rather meet a roaring lion in a narrow path than a well-intentioned man who was ignorant. We must at least be as well informed as the average intelligent layman, and no parochial activities can excuse a mind barren of thought and a study table which holds nothing heavier than a book of "Little Sermons for every Sunday in the Christian Year."[2]

It is related of the author of *Onward, Christian Soldiers* that his bishop objected to the line, "With the Cross of Jesus going on before," as savoring of Romish practices.

---

[1] From *H. R. L. Sheppard, Life and Letters*, by R. Ellis Roberts, John Murray (London, 1942).
[2] From *The Human Parson*, Morehouse-Gorham (New York, 1929); John Murray (London, 1924).

He replied by suggesting the alteration: "With the Cross of Jesus left behind the door." The bishop surrendered.[3]

I heard a story the other day of a group of men who were traveling home by train. One of them, in a corner of the carriage, was busy with a crossword puzzle. Suddenly he looked up.

"A word of three letters, with 'o' in the middle meaning man's best friend?" he inquired.

"Dog," chorused everybody. And if you were asked the same question, that's almost certainly the word that would come first to your mind. But it didn't quite fit into the puzzle.

"I think," said the man with the pencil, "that the last letter must be 'd.'"

But still he couldn't see it. And neither apparently could any of his companions. Or, if they did, they didn't like to suggest anything so revolutionary.

Yet surely man's best and most tolerant friend is God.[4]

GOD HAS A SENSE OF HUMOR

It would go pretty hard with most of us if we lost our sense of humor, for just now and then we must either laugh or howl.

Some people cannot laugh today, for there is nothing in their world to laugh about.

You cannot expect the unemployed father of a family to see anything but the grimmest humor—which is no fun at all—when he is told that many thousands of pounds are to be expended on an Eat More Bread crusade. But those whose health and work hold, may still be invited to grin as well as to bear their inflictions.

Humor can ease ugly situations, smooth rough corners, and enable men to grasp life's nettle firmly with a power that is more than human.

A good joke may be a perfect work of art, of divine service to every pilgrim on the road of life.

---

[3] From *God and My Neighbor*, Cassell and Co., Ltd. (London, 1937).
[4] *Ibid.*

Why may we cry but not laugh in church, sing but not smile, look pompous but not pleased?

Except that the record of humor is not always clean and in some of its guffawing or giggling forms still in the stage of savagery, there is no excuse for leaving it out of our religion.

Surely it is unbelievable that God lacks what so often refreshes and recreates His children; or that the Creator is without that which His creatures delight to possess.

It is to me unthinkable that Jesus Christ, who told stories so charmingly, refrained from making children laugh, or that there was no playfulness in His speech when, for instance, He described the camel, hump and all, sliding unnoticed down the throat of the Pharisee.

Did no one in the crowd smile?

Laughter may be cruel and unspeakably ugly, but humor is divinely useful—a perfect work of art, so far as it goes.

There is a little prayer I use every day of my life that was originally an exquisite joke, consciously or unconsciously made.

It is the best modern prayer I know.

The joke may be familiar, but, as the prayer is not, I ask leave to tell them both.

In Mesopotamia during the war a certain soldier who was up to his neck in dirt and danger, received a letter from home of a nasty, nagging and unpleasant character.

It was the fair limit—more than human nature, in circumstances so horrible, could stand.

Back went an answer which, after asking that he might never again receive such an epistle, ended with this naïve and delightful request:—

"For God's sake, let me enjoy this 'ere war in peace."

If you know a better prayer for what we all need, internal peace, even if there must be external tumult, I should be glad to know of it.

Let me enjoy this 'ere war in peace. Life still is, and always will be, a war for most of us, but the Father of Jesus Christ can give the Peace that passeth all understanding with which we may carry on even happily. It is through, not from, trouble that we need to be saved.[5]

---
[5] From *Some of My Religion*, Harper & Brothers (New York, 1936).

NO SOAP

On two occasions the King encouraged us by his presence. Just before His Majesty's first visit I mislaid the notes of my short address. I had to go into the pulpit without them and my embarrassment on arriving was not diminished by spotting my manuscript where I must have dropped it, alongside the service paper which had been placed in the front pew for His Majesty's use. I have often had occasion to regret my illegible handwriting, but I think it served me well that day for the first reminder on those notes stood as follows: "Loyal and sincere gratitude to H. M., *but no soap*."[6]

LET US GO A-WHOOFING

Some years ago we were all told that we must get brighter and brighter! We were to be gay: "A Brighter London" was the slogan. It was suggested that we should dance on the green, hang carpets out of the windows, at times of exuberance, get a maypole stuck up in the churchyard and sing folk songs and roundelays with curious old names such as "Oh, let us go a-whoofing." We did not know what whoofing meant: spoofing would have done just as well, I imagine, provided it was done in harmony and, of course, "ryghte merrilee." It seemed for a time that religion was largely a matter of whoofing. Anyhow, of course, we at St. Martin's were not going to be out of it. We too would be merry. We would whoof with the best of them. Trust the Vicar for that! But how and when and where? What better than a little caroling early on May Day morning and on the tower of St. Martin's, reminiscent of the charm of Magdalen? No sooner thought than arranged. A fine array of talent, and a good deal of it offered their services: the English Singers, Steuart Wilson, and a host of others. The Press was called in and told the citizens of London of the treat in store. We would send them whoofing to their work up the breezy heights of Ludgate Hill early on May morning. When the day arrived, I rose with the lark, to be Queen of the May, having hardly slept the night before for excitement. Certainly it was a bad-looking day, very wet and very windy; still, all the more was caroling needed. I went

---

[6] From *H. R. L. Sheppard, Life and Letters,* by R. Ellis Roberts, John Murray (London, 1942).

over to the church in a greatcoat and scarf, and found a fine muster of singers, cold but full of bravery and goodwill. I found, too, a vast crowd of citizens, to which the police objected, blocking the space between the church and the National Gallery and extending well into the Square. I stood on the steps and made a cheery speech to the crowd while the singers wended their way up aloft. It was a gay speech all about Merrie England and May Day and, of course, whoofing; I told them that at any moment now a lovely sound would burst on their ears from the tower above. I was very cold, but I cast away greatcoat and scarf to show that it was May morning, and I shouted to an ever-increasing crowd in the teeth of a howling gale. There was a delay up above, so I began to talk again, suggesting to the citizens that they had better put up their umbrellas, that was, if they could. (I called it a "passing shower with an enheartening breeze.") The delay went on, so I filled up the time by talking once more of the joy of whoofing, sending messengers up to the tower by the score to ask why the dickens the singing hadn't begun. Then the crowd began. They made noises more like hoofing than whoofing, and in despair I dashed up the tower in person to find out what was wrong. Halfway up, I was borne back and down by the weight of a vast crowd of hot and perspiring minstrels. When we landed in a heap at the bottom to the unpleasing sounds of the crowd without, I asked with some show of temper, why in heaven's name they hadn't done their whoofing. "Whoofing," they shrieked, "we've been at it for half an hour; couldn't you hear it?" Not a sound had penetrated below! I did not return to the citizens to explain. I walked quickly through the church and got home by the back door, and then crept to the study window to look through the curtains. I watched the citizens dispersing and a more whoofless and unlovely lot I never beheld.[7]

On the afternoon of the day on which I was ordained a deacon I was traveling to my work in East London. There were two drunken working men as my near neighbors—the one had reached a stage that rendered him ferocious, the other was well disposed to a degree that was almost maudlin.

On catching sight of me the former remarked: "There's a ——

[7] *Ibid.*

parson!" but the other, full of genial intention, stopped him. "Now, George, don't blame him—it's not 'is fault. It's 'ard luck, that's what I says."[8]

---

[8] From *The Human Parson*, Morehouse-Gorham (New York, 1929); John Murray (London, 1924).

39. SPARKS

I do love Christmas—to me it is like a Gothic ruin come to life for twenty-four hours.

I'm hard pressed for personal income, but always have charitable money.

Not till the devil's cause gets hold of men by their virtues and consciences, as well as by their pride and prejudices, does it become really dangerous.[1]

The first concern of those who would be Christians should not be to add their name to the roll of members of any Church or Chapel, but to adventure on their own in the difficult business of Christian living.

It is intolerable that Christianity should bless the gutter and leave men in it.

Are we to blame the Christian God, because, having built our civilization on a basis which our Lord said would lead to collapse, we see around us everywhere signs of disintegration?

I wonder how we must appear to those who watch us and hear us making our brave assertions about the Fatherhood of God, the brotherhood of man, and our personal devotion to the Lord Christ. I wonder

---
[1] From *What Can We Believe?* edited by Laurence Housman, Jonathan Cape (London, 1939).

if we do not seem to them like Alpine climbers who, having greased their faces and covered them with masks, and having put on their nailed boots, and taken ice axes in their hands, then proceed to walk gravely up the mild heights of Ludgate Hill?

I can more easily see our Lord sweeping the streets of London, than issuing edicts from its cathedral.

I am afraid there is often more real fellowship in the public house than in the Christian Church.

In idle moments I have wondered whether it would be possible to persuade old gentlemen who haunt West End clubs to march gallantly in procession—four by four—through the streets of Mayfair, and I have come to the conclusion that there are only two causes that might compel them to take part in a proceeding so conspicuous and ungentlemanly. One, of course, would be their protest against a Measure of Prohibition; and the other, I think, would be for the defense of "Our dear old Church," against any political attack on its Establishments and Endowments.[2]

We have played for safety, position and Prestige too long. . . . We have been content to provide a peephole through which people could see God through a blizzard.

Any idea that a round collar is a slipped halo must be once and for all abandoned.[3]

[2] From *The Impatience of a Parson*, Harper & Brothers (New York, 1927).
[3] From *Some of My Religion*, Harper & Brothers (New York, 1936).

JAY